CW00675783

PENGUIN BO
RAIN IN THE MOU

Ruskin Bond was born in Kasauli, Himachal Pradesh, in 1934, and grew up in Jamnagar (Gujarat), Dehradun and Shimla. In the course of a writing career spanning thirty-five years, he has written over a hundred short stories, essays, novels and more than thirty books for children. Three collections of the short stories, *The Night Train at Deoli, Time Stops at Shamli* and *Our Trees Still Grow in Dehra* have been published by Penguin India. He has also edited two anthologies, *The Penguin Book of Indian Ghost Stories* and *The Penguin Book of Indian Railway Storeis.*

The Room on the Roof was his first novel, written when he was seventeen, and it received the John Llewellyn Rhys Memorial Prize in 1957. *Vagrants in the Valley* was also written in his teens and picks up from where *The Room on the Roof* leaves off.

These two novellas were published in one volume by Penguin India in 1993 and in early 1995 a collection of stories, essays, poems and a novella were brought out in a volume titled *Delhi Is Not Far: The Best of Ruskin Bond.*

Ruskin Bond received the Sahitya Akademi Award for English writing in India for 1992, for *Our Trees Still Grow in Dehra.*

Books by the same author

Fiction

The Room on the Roof and Vagrants in the Valley
Night Train at Deoli & Other Stories
Time Stops at Shamli & Other Stories
Our Trees Still Grow in Dehra (Stories)
The Penguin Book of Indian Ghost Stories (Edited)

Children's Books

Panther's Moon & Other Stories
The Room on the Roof

RAIN
IN THE
MOUNTAINS

*Notes
from the
Himalayas*

**RUSKIN
BOND**

PENGUIN BOOKS

PENGUIN BOOKS
Published by the Penguin Group
Penguin Books India Pvt. Ltd, 11 Community Centre, Panchsheel Park,
New Delhi 110 017, India
Penguin Group (USA) Inc., 375 Hudson Street, New York, New York 10014,
USA
Penguin Group (Canada), 90 Eglinton Avenue East, Suite 700, Toronto,
Ontario, M4P 2Y3, Canada (a division of Pearson Penguin Canada Inc.)
Penguin Books Ltd, 80 Strand, London WC2R 0RL, England
Penguin Ireland, 25 St Stephen's Green, Dublin 2, Ireland (a division of Penguin
Books Ltd)
Penguin Group (Australia), 250 Camberwell Road, Camberwell, Victoria
3124, Australia (a division of Pearson Australia Group Pty Ltd)
Penguin Group (NZ), 67 Apollo Drive, Rosedale, Auckland 0632,
New Zealand (a division of Pearson New Zealand Ltd)
Penguin Group (South Africa) (Pty) Ltd, 24 Sturdee Avenue, Rosebank,
Johannesburg 2196, South Africa

Penguin Books Ltd, Registered Offices: 80 Strand, London WC2R 0RL,
England

First published in Viking by Penguin Books India 1993
Published in Penguin Books India 1996

Copyright © Ruskin Bond 1993

All rights reserved

24 23 22 21 20 19

ISBN 9780140236910

This is a work of fiction. Names, characters, places and incidents are either the
product of the author's imagination or are used fictitiously, and any resemblance
to any actual person, living or dead, events or locales is entirely coincidental.

Typeset in Palatino by FOLIO, New Delhi
Printed at Shri Krishna Printers, Noida

This book is sold subject to the condition that it shall not, by way of trade or
otherwise, be lent, resold, hired out, or otherwise circulated without the
publisher's prior written consent in any form of binding or cover other than
that in which it is published and without a similar condition including this
condition being imposed on the subsequent purchaser and without limiting
the rights under copyright reserved above, no part of this publication may be
reproduced, stored in or introduced into a retrieval system, or transmitted in
any form or by any means (electronic, mechanical, photocopying, recording
or otherwise), without the prior written permission of both the copyright owner
and the above-mentioned publisher of this book.

For
David Davidar,
who gave me the concept
for this book

Acknowledgements

ALL THE ESSAYS in Sections II and III of this book have appeared, at various times, in *The Christian Science Monitor* (Boston).

Many of them also appeared in *The Hindu, The Hindustan Times, The Telegraph, The Times of India, The Statesman, The Tribune, The Pioneer, Deccan Herald, The Economic Times, Sunday Mid-Day, The Independent, Financial Express, The Lady* (London), *School* (Australia), *Cricket* (USA) and *The Asia Magazine* (Hong Kong).

Some articles also appeared in magazines that have since closed down. These were: *Blackwood's* (London and Edinburgh), *Hemisphere* (Australia), and *The Heritage* (Madras).

'Once Upon a Mountain Time', 'Miss Bun and others', 'Time to Close the Window' and the play 'It Must be the Mountains' have not appeared in print before.

Some of the poems are also appearing here for the first time. A number of them were published by the Writers Workshop (Calcutta), *Hemisphere* (Australia), and *Blackwood's Magazine*.

*

Illustrations by Vinita Chand

Prologue

Aᴸᴸ ɴɪɢʜᴛ ᴛʜᴇ rain has been drumming on the corrugated tin roof. There has been no storm, no thunder, just the steady swish of a tropical downpour. It helps me to lie awake; at the same time, it doesn't keep me from sleeping.

It is a good sound to read by—the rain outside, the quiet within—and, although tin roofs are given to springing unaccountable leaks, there is a feeling of being untouched by, and yet in touch with, the rain.

*

When, at the age of seventeen, I went to live in Jersey (in the Channel Islands), my first job was that of a junior clerk in a solicitor's office. The firm, believe it or not, was called Smith, Smith and Smith, but it was unusual to find all the partners in the office at the same time. The telephone would ring, and the ensuing conversation would go like this:

> 'May I speak to Mr Smith?'
> 'I'm sorry, he's away on holiday.'
> 'Then may I speak to Mr Smith?'
> 'He just went out to lunch.'
> 'Well, never mind. May I speak to Mr Smith?'
> 'Speaking.'

I left this firm to work for a well-known travel agency, which had just decided to set up a small branch office in Jersey. It was manned, or rather womanned, by a certain Mrs Manning, who had left her husband on the mainland and was busy having an affair with a man who renovated old fire-extinguishers and sold them as new. She took me on as her assistant, and then left me to man the telephone, make hotel reservations, and keep in touch with the head office while she had the time of her life. Being totally inexperienced in this line of work, I made a complete mess of everything, for I had yet to appreciate the difference between Twin Beds and Double Beds. People who had never slept together were booked into rooms with double-beds, while those who had shared the same bed for years were now forced to sleep separately. Mrs Manning and I both got the sack.

My third job consisted of carrying pay-packets down to workers in the island's ancient sewers. Actually, there was a literary connection here, because Victor Hugo (who had lived on the islands for some time), had apparently visited them in order to collect 'atmosphere' for his novels. They certainly had atmosphere.

But why am I telling you all this? This is a book about my life in the Himalayan foothills.

Well, when I finally got back to India, I felt I'd had enough of doing uncongenial work and that henceforth I would make a living from freelance writing.

I could not immediately take to the mountains, but from my small flat in Dehradun I began bombarding every newspaper and magazine editor in the land with articles, stories, essays and even poems. In those days there were hardly any book publishers around (apart from those who brought out text-books), so that one really had to concentrate on journalism. There was, of course, *The Statesman* and *The Illustrated Weekly* and a couple of other well-known papers; and there was also *The Tribune* of Ambala (it shifted to Chandigarh in the 1960s), and *The Leader* of Allahabad, and *Shankar's Weekly*, and Baburao Patel's *Mother India* and *The Hindu's Sport and Pastime*, which actually published fiction along with its sports features. *Mother India* was not about motherhood, it was about Baburao Patel, who solved your personal problems along with the world's problems in each monthly issue. Payments varied from five to fifty rupees per article, but for several years I managed to eke out a living as a freelance. That man is strongest who stands alone!

This was in the Fifties and Sixties. Things got better in the

Seventies. I discovered *The Christian Science Monitor* in Boston, *Blackwood's* in Edinburgh, and *The Asia Magazine* in Hong Kong, and I was able to realize my dream of living in the hills. My children's books began to be published in different parts of the world, too, and then in the Eighties along came Penguin India. When they expressed an interest in publishing some of my work, I was, like a good boy scout, 'fully prepared'! Those hundreds of stories and essays and poems and sketches were all there, just waiting to be collected and published between beautiful covers. And people even bought my books, thus proving wrong those Jeremiahs who had always said my work would never 'sell'! Of course, more people are reading books than ever before in spite of, or possibly because of, the TV–video boom. The lack of any thought-content in these soap operas is driving intelligent people back to literature.

So how did this book come about?

The journals, the diary extracts, the play and even some of the essays and poems have not been published before. But they were lying in one of my boxes, forgotten for many years until Boston University offered to keep my papers in their Special Collections Library. Going through those old diaries and exercise books again, I thought they made, if not a complete, then a fairly entertaining record of the twenty-five years or more that I have spent here on the mountain-top. When I showed them to David Davidar, he suggested that if I linked them up with my personal and nature essays and poems, they would make a book of some substance.

I think I should explain that the book is divided into five sections. The first section has the journals written in the Seventies and ends with a play written about the same time. The second section contains some of my essays written in the Sixties, Seventies, and Eighties; these are followed by the third section which are diary extracts. The fourth section is a selection of essays written in the Nineties. Section five, the Epilogue, ends the book.

Some of my poems were jotted down as spontaneous diary entries, so that they are almost nature notes in themselves. We felt that a selection would not be out of place here.

I couldn't have done it without his help and the guidance and support of his colleagues, especially Rima Handa, who has arranged everything so neatly, in order to make this book a complete reading experience.

*

Bells in the hills. A school-bell ringing, and children's voices drifting through an open window. A temple bell heard faintly from across the valley. Heavy silver ankle bells on the feet of sturdy hill women. Sheep bells heard high up on the mountainside.

There are sounds that come from a distance, beautiful because they are far away, voices on the wind—'they walketh upon the wings of the wind.' Drums beating rhythmically in a forest clearing. The croaking of frogs from the rainwater pond behind the house.

And so we return to the rain, with which my favourite sounds began. I have sat out in the open at night, after a shower of rain, when the whole air is murmuring and tinkling with the voices of crickets and grasshoppers and little frogs. There is one melodious sound, a sweet repeated trill, that I have never been able to trace to its source. Perhaps it is a little tree frog, or it may be a small green cricket. I shall never know. There is so much that we shall never know. Ah, sweet mystery of life!

Contents

ONCE
UPON A
MOUNTAIN
TIME

*Pages
from a
Journal*

Once Upon a Mountain Time

My solitude is not my own, for I see now how much it belongs to them—and that I have a responsibility for it in their regard, not just in my own. It is because I am one with them that I owe it to them to be alone, and when I am alone they are not 'they' but my own self. There are no strangers!

From *Confessions of a Guilty Bystander*
—Thomas Merton

THE TREES STAND watch over my day-to-day life. They are the guardians of my conscience. I have no one else to answer to, so I live and work under the generous but highly principled supervision of the trees—especially the deodars, who stand on guard, unbending, on the slope above the cottage. The oak and maples are a little more tolerant, they have had to put up with a great deal, their branches continually lopped for fuel and fodder. 'What would *they* think?' I ask myself on many a occasion. 'What would they like me to do?' And I do what *I* think they would approve of most!

Well, it's nice to have someone to turn to . . . .

The leaves are a fresh pale green in the spring rain. I can look at the trees from my window—look down on them almost, because the window is on the first floor of the cottage, and the hillside runs away at a sharp angle into the ravine. The trees and I know each other quite intimately, and we have much to say to each other from time to time.

I do nearly all my writing at this window-seat. The trees watch over me as I write. Whenever I look up, they remind me that they are there. They are my best critics. As long as I am aware of their presence, I can try to avoid the trivial and the banal.

Ramesh, the son of the municipal cleaner, looms darkly in the doorway. He is a stunted boy with a large head, but has wide gentle eyes. His orange-coloured trousers brighten up the surrounding gloom.

'What do you want, Ramesh?'

'Newspapers.'

'To sell to the kabari?'

'No. For wrapping my school-books.'

'Well, take a few.' I give him half a dozen old newspapers, the headlines already look meaningless. 'Sit down and wait for it to stop raining.'

He sits awkwardly on a mora.

'And what is your cousin Vinod doing these days?' (Vinod is a good-looking ne'er-do-well who seldom does anything apart from hanging around cinema halls.)

'Nothing.'

'Doesn't he go to school?'

'He has stopped going to school. He got a job at fifty rupees a month, but he left after a week. He says he will join the army in September.'

The rain stops and Ramesh departs. The clouds begin to break up, the sun strikes the steep hill on my left. A woman is chopping up sticks. I hear the tinkle of cow-bells. Water drips from a leaking drain-pipe. And suddenly, clear and pure, the song of the whistling-thrush emerges like a dark sweet secret from the depths of the ravine.

*

Bijju is back from school and is taking his parents' cattle out to graze. He sees me at the window and waves, then grabs his favourite cow Neelu by the tail and tells her to hurry up.

Bijju is twelve, a fair, good-looking Garhwali boy. His younger sister and brother are very pretty children. The father, an electrician, is a rather self-effacing man. The mother is a strong, hard woman. I have watched her on the hillside cutting grass. She has the muscular calves of a man, solid feet and heavy hands; but she is a handsome woman. They live in a rented outhouse further up the hill.

4

Bijju doesn't visit me very often. He is rather shy. But one day I looked out of the window and there he was in the branches of the oak tree, smiling at me rather hesitantly. We spoke to each other across the three or four yards that separate house from oak tree.

'If I jump, I can land in your tree,' I said.

'And if I jump I will be in your house,' said Bijju.

'Come on then, jump!'

But he shook his head. He was afraid of me. The tree was safe. He put his arms round the thickest branch and held himself close to it. He looked very right in the tree, as though he belonged there, a boy of the woods, a tree-spirit peeping out from a house of glossy new leaves.

'Come on, jump!'

'*You* jump,' he said.

In the evening his sister brings the cows home. I meet her on the path above the house. She is only a year younger than Bijju, a very bonny girl who is going to be ravishingly beautiful when she grows up, if they don't marry her off too soon. She too has the same timid smile. But if these children are timid of humans, they are not afraid in the forest, and often wander far afield with Neelu the blue cow and others. (And S, who is eighteen and educated at an English-medium private school, wouldn't go alone into the forest if you paid him!) But the trees know their own. They will cherish the wild spirits and frighten the daylight out of the tame.

*

The whistling-thrush is here, bathing in the rain-water puddle beneath the window. He loves this spot. So now, when there is no rain, I fill the puddle with water, just so that my favourite bird keeps coming.

His bath finished, he perches on a branch of the walnut tree. His glossy blue-black wings glitter in the sunshine. At any moment he will start singing.

Here he goes! He tries out the tune, whistling to himself, and then, confident of the notes, sends his thrilling full-throated voice far over the forest. The song dies down, trembling,

5

lingering in the air; starts again, joyfully, and then suddenly stops, as though the singer had forgotten the words or the tune.

*

Vinod, the ne'er-do-well, turns up with a friend, asking me to give them some work. They want to go to the pictures but have no money.

'You can dig up this slope below the house,' I tell them. 'The soil is good for growing vegetables.

This sounds too much like hard work for Vinod, who says, 'We'll come and do it tomorrow.'

'No, we'll do it now,' says his more enterprising friend, and to my surprise they set to work.

Now and then I look out of the window. They are digging away with fair enthusiasm.

After about half an hour, Vinod keeps sitting down for short rests, to the increasing irritation of his partner. They are soon snapping at each other. Vinod looks very funny when he sulks, because he has a snub nose, and somehow a snub nose and a ferocious expression only reminds me of Richmal Crompton's William. But the work gets done by evening and they are quite pleased with their earnings.

*

Bijju is right at the top of a big oak. The branches sway to his movements. He grins down at me and waves. The higher he is in the tree, the more confident he becomes. It is only when he is down on the ground that he becomes shy and speechless.

He has allowed the cows to wander, and presently his mother's deep voice can be heard calling, 'Neelu, Neelu!' (The other cows don't have names.) And then: 'Where is that wretched boy?'

*

Sir Edmund Gibson has come up. He spends the summer in the big house just down the road. He is wheezing a lot and says he has water in his lungs—and who wouldn't, at the age of eighty-six.

'Ruskin, my advice to you,' he says, 'is never to live beyond the age of eighty.'

'Well, once ought to be enough, sir.'

He is a big man, but not as red in the face as he used to be. His Gurkha manservant, Tirlok, has to push him up the steep slope to my gate.

Sir Edmund was once the British Resident in the Kathiawar states. He knew my parents in Jamnagar, when I was just five or six. He is a bachelor and is looked after by his servants.

His farm at Ramgarh doesn't make any money and he will probably give it to his retainers.

When Sir Edmund was Resident, he was once shot at from close range by a terrorist. The man took four shots and missed every time. He must have been a terrible shot, or perhaps the pistol was faulty, because Sir E presents a very large target.

He also treasures two letters from Mahatma Gandhi, which were written from prison.

'I liked Gandhi,' says Sir E. 'He had a sense of humour. No politician today has a sense of humour. They all take themselves far too seriously. But not Gandhi. He took his work seriously, but not himself. When I went to see him in prison, I asked him if he was comfortable, and he smiled and said, "Even if I was, I wouldn't admit it!"'

Sir E's servant brings tea, but there isn't any milk. I think I have exhausted Bijju's supply.

Now it's dusk and the trees are very still, very quiet. Far away I can hear the chuk-chuk-chuk of a nightjar. The lights on Landour hill come on, one by one. Prem is singing in the kitchen. There is a whirr of wings as the king-crows fly into the trees to roost for the night. A rustling in the dry leaves below the window. A snake? Field rats? Porcupines? It is now too dark to find out. The day has ended, and the trees move closer together in the dark.

*

We are treated to one of those spectacular electric storms which are fairly frequent at this time of the year, late spring or early summer. The clouds grow very dark, then send bolts of lightning sizzling across the sky, lighting up the entire range of mountains. When the storm is directly overhead, there is hardly a pause in the frequency of the lightning; it is like a bright light being switched on and off with barely a second's interruption.

John Lang, writing in Dickens's magazine *Household Words* in 1853, almost exactly 120 years ago, had this to say about one of our storms:

> I have seen a storm on the heights of Jura—such a storm as Lord Byron describes. I have seen lightning, and heard thunder in Australia; I have, off Tierra del Fuego, the Cape of Good Hope, and the coast of Java, kept watch in thunderstorms which have drowned in their roaring the human voice, and made everyone deaf and stupefied; but these storms are not to be compared with a thunderstorm at Mussoorie or Landour.

Forgotten today, Lang was a popular writer in the mid-nineteenth century. He was also a successful barrister, who represented the Rani of Jhansi in her litigation with the East India Company. He spent his last years in Mussoorie and was buried in the Camel's Back cemetery. His grave proved to be almost as elusive as his books and I found it with some difficulty, overgrown with moss and periwinkle. Prem and I cleaned it up until the inscription stood out quite clearly.

Prem won't come home on a stormy night like this. He is afraid of the dark, but more than that, he is afraid of thunderstorms. It is as though the gods are ganging up against him. So he will spend the night in the school quarters, where he is visiting his mother who is staying there with relatives. In the morning he will turn up with a sheepish grin, saying it got very late and he didn't want to wake me in the middle of the night.

*

In the morning he turns up with a sheepish grin, saying it got very late and he didn't want to wake me in the middle of the night.

I try to feign anger, but it is a gloriously fresh and spirited morning; impossible to feel angry. A strong breeze is driving the clouds away, and the sun keeps breaking through The birds are particularly active. The king-crows (who weren't here last year), seem to have taken up residence in the oaks. I don't know why they are called crows. They are slim elegant black birds, with long forked tails, and their call, far from being a caw, is quite musical, though slightly metallic. The mynahs are very busy, very noisy, looking for a nesting site in the roof. The babblers are raking over fallen leaves, snapping up absent-minded grasshoppers. Now and then, the whistling-thrush bursts into song, and then all other bird sounds pale into insignificance. Bijju has taken his cows to pasture and now scrambles up the hill, heading for home; he is late for school, and that is why he is in a hurry. He waves to me.

Both he and Prem have the high cheek-bones and the deep-set eyes of the hill people. Prem, of course, is tall and dark. Bijju is small and fair; but he will grow into a sturdy young fellow.

The rain has driven the scorpions out of their rocks and crevices. I found one sitting on a loaf of bread. Up came his sting when we disturbed him. Prem tipped him out on the veranda steps and he scurried off into the bushes. I do not kill insects and other small creatures if I can help it, but there is a limit to my hospitality. I spared a centipede yesterday even though, last year, I was bitten by one which had occupied the seat of my pyjamas. Our hill scorpions and centipedes are not as dangerous as those found in the plains, and probably the same can be said for the people.

Prem tells me that his uncle is immune to scorpion stings, and allows himself to be stung in order to demonstrate his immunity. Apparently his mother was stung by a scorpion shortly before his birth!

Azure butterflies flit about the garden like flakes of sky.

Learnt two new words:

bosky = wooded, bushy (bosky shadows); girding = jesting,

jeering (girding schoolboys, girding monkeys).

*

Poor old Sir E is in a bad way. He has diarrhoea, and little or no control over the muscles that play a part in controlling the bowels. The Gurkha servant called me, and I went over with some tablets. Sir E looked quite exhausted and was panting from the exertion of walking from his bed to the toilet. The Gurkha is very good—gives Sir E his bath, dresses him, helps him on with his pyjamas.

Grateful for my alacrity in coming over with some medicine, Sir E offers me a whisky and soda (the first time he has ever done this), and pours himself a stiff brandy. He dozes off now and then, but the laboured breathing won't stop. He is a tough old tree, but I think he is beginning to find his massive frame something of a burden.

I make an attempt at conversation.

'Were you at Oxford or Cambridge?'

'Oxford. I joined Oxford in 1905 and left in 1909. Came out to India in 1910.'

He has an excellent memory, unlike Mr Biggs (a retired headmaster) who is ten years younger but will repeat the same story thrice in ten minutes.

'And when were you knighted?' I ask.

'1939 or 1940.'

He is too tired to do much talking. I let him doze off, and give my attention to the whisky. The log fire burns well, the flames cast their glow on Sir E's white hair and hanging jowls. The stertorous breathing grows in volume. He wakes up suddenly, complains that the fire is too hot; Tirlok opens the window. I finish the whisky; he doesn't offer another. It is his supper time, anyway, and I suggest soup and toast. 'Call me in the night if you have any trouble,' I say. He looks very grateful. The loneliness must press upon him a great deal.

I go out into the night. The trees are bending to a strong wind. From the foliage comes a deep sigh, the voice of leagues of trees sleeping and half disturbed in their sleep. The sky is clear, tremendous with stars.

*

For the first time this year I hear the barbet, a sure sign the summer is upon us. Its importunate cry carries far across the hills. It can keep this up for hours, like a beggar. Indeed, its plaint—*unneow, unneow!*—has been likened in the hills to that of the spirit of the village moneylender who has died before he can collect his dues. (*'Unneow!'* is a cry for justice!)

It is difficult to spot the barbet. It is a fat green bird (no bigger than a myna, but fatter), and it usually perches at the very top of a deodar or cypress.

The whistling-thrush comes to bathe in the rainwater puddle.

Sir E is much better and is sitting outside in the shade of an old oak. They are probably about the same age. What a rugged constitution this man must have; first, to survive, as a young man, all those diseases such as cholera, typhoid, dysentery, malaria, even the plague, which carried off so many Europeans in India (including my father); and now, an old man, to live and battle with congested lungs, a bad heart, weak eyes, bad teeth, recalcitrant bowels, and god knows what else, and still be able to derive some pleasure from living. His old Hillman car is equally indestructible. But, like Sir E, it can't get up the hill any more; he uses it only in Dehradun.

I think his longevity is due simply to the fact that he refuses to go to bed when he is unwell. No amount of diarrhoea, or water in his lungs, will prevent him from getting up, dressing, writing letters, or getting on with the latest Wodehouse (a contemporary of his) or *Blackwood's Magazine*, to which he has been subscribing for the last fifty years! He was pleased to find that some of my own essays were appearing in *Blackwood's*. Nothing will keep him from his 4 o'clock tea or his evening whisky and soda. He is determined, I am sure, to die in his chair, with all his clothes on. The thought of being taken unawares while still in his pyjamas must be something of a nightmare to him.

(His favourite film, he once told me, was *They Died With Their Boots On*.)

*

The cicadas are tuning up for their first summer concert. Even Mrs Biggs, who is hard of hearing, can hear them.

Yesterday I met her on the road above the cottage and exchanged pleasantries. Up at Wynberg the girls' choir was hard at practice.

'The girls are in good voice today,' I remarked.

'Oh yes, Mr Bond,' she said, presuming I meant the cicadas. 'They do it with their legs, don't they?'

A week in Delhi. It is still only early summer, but the heat almost knocks one over. Slept on a roof, along with thousands of mosquitoes. It cools off in the early hours, but only briefly, before the sun comes shouting over the rooftops. The dust lies thick on floors, leaves, books, people. May's golden dust!

Now, back in the hills, I am struck first of all by the silence. The house, too, makes itself felt. It has been here too long not to have acquired a personality of its own. It is not a cheerful looking place, nor is it exactly gloomy. My bedroom is rather dark, (because it faces the abrupt slope of the hillside) but there is a wild cherry growing just outside the window—a cherry tree which I nurtured ever since it was a tiny seedling, five or six years ago, and which has now grown so tall that the branches tap against the roof whenever there is a breeze. It is a funny sort of cherry because it flowers in November instead of in the spring like other fruit trees. Small birds and small boys willingly eat the berries, which are too acid for adult palates.

The sitting-room, with its two big windows looking out on the forest, is a bright room. Most of the wall space is taken up by my books. The rugs are worn and tattered—they have been with the house right from the beginning, I think—and I can't afford new ones.

> *On books and friends I spend my money;*
> *For stones and bricks I haven't any.*

Sir E, quite recovered from his recent illness, has gone down to Dehra again to attend to his farm and the demands of his farm workers. He should be back at the end of the month.

The brilliant blue-black of the whistling-thrush shows up best when the sun is glinting off its back, but this seldom happens, because the bird likes to keep to the shade where it is almost black. Hopping about, it reminds me of Fred Astaire dancing in top hat and tails.

Now that it's getting hot, my small pool attracts a number of afternoon visitors—the mynahs, babblers, a bulbul, a magpie. After their dip they perch in the cherry tree to dry themselves and I can watch them without getting up from my bed, where I take an afternoon siesta. I reserve the afternoons for doing nothing. 'Silence and non-action are the root of all things,' says Tao. Especially on a drowsy afternoon.

But I haven't seen the whistling-thrush for several days. Perhaps he is offended at having to share the pool which he was the first to discover. I haven't heard his song either, which probably means that he has moved down to the stream where it is cooler and shadier.

*

Prem's mother and younger sister come for a few days. His mother is a very quiet woman and doesn't say much even to her son. She is quite handsome, although she looks rather worn and tired, due probably to her recent illness.

His little sister, about four, is a friendly little gazelle; not in the least pretty, but lively and intelligent. She will have to stay here for at least six months to be properly treated for her incipient tuberculosis. There is no treatment to be had in their village.

While I am resting, still exhausted from an attack of hill dysentery (who called this a health resort?), Sir E blows in, red-faced, as distressed as a stranded whale. His Gurkha servant has walked out, after quarrelling with his wife and mother-in-law, and has taken with him his twin sons (aged one and a half). I calm Sir E, tell him Tirlok will be back in a day or two—he is probably trying to show how indispensable he is!

Sir E takes out a cigarette and strikes a match, and the entire match-box flares up, burning a finger. Definitely not his day. I apply Burnol.

'It's all that damned girl's fault,' he says. 'She has a vile temper, just like her mother. We were very wise not to marry, Ruskin.'

Wise or not, I seem to have acquired a family all the same.

Hundreds of white butterflies are flitting through the forest.

*

When Prem told his mother that I kept a human skull in my sitting-room (given to me by Anil, a medical student, and *not* ɼ inched from the cemetery as some suppose), she told him not to spend too much time near it. If he did, he would be possessed by the spirit of the woman who had originally inhabited the skull.

But Prem, at the present time, is immune to spirits, having succumbed to the charms of his young wife who stays downstairs with his mother. They have only been married a few months. He leans over the balcony, chatting with her; advises her on how to keep the courtyard clean; then makes her a small broom from the twigs of a wild honeysuckle bush. She enjoys all the attention she is getting.

The sky is overcast this morning. Dust from the plains has formed a thick haze which hides the valley and the mountains. We are badly in need of rain. Down in the plains, over 200 people have died of heatstroke.

I haven't seen Bijju for some days, but this morning his sister, Binya, was out with the cows. What a sturdy little girl she is; and pretty, too. I will write a story about her.*

*

'We'll take you to the pictures one day, Sir Edmund.'

'Yes, I must see one more picture before I die.'

So there comes a time when we start thinking in terms of the

---

* This story was called 'The Blue Umbrella'.

last picture, the last book, the last visit, the last party. But Sir E's remark is matter-of-fact. He is given to boredom but not to melancholy. And he has a timeless quality. I have noticed this in other old people; they look more permanent than the young.

He sums it all up by saying, 'I don't mind being dead, but I shall miss being alive.'

*

A number of small birds are here to bathe and drink in the little pool beneath the cherry tree: hunting-parties of tits—grey tits, red-headed tits and green-backed tits, and two delicate little willow warblers. They take turns in the pool. While the green-backs are taking a plunge, the red-heads wait patiently on the moss-covered rocks, coming down later to sip daintily at the edge of the pool; they don't like getting their feet wet! Finally, when they have all gone away, the whistling-thrush arrives and indulges in an orgy of bathing, as he now has the entire pool to himself.

The babblers are adept at snapping up the little garden skinks that scuttle about in the leaves and grass. The skinks are quite brittle and are easily broken to pieces with a few hard raps of the beak. Then down they go! Babblers are also good at sifting through dead leaves and seizing upon various insects.

The honeybees push their way through the pursed lips of the antirrhinum and disappear completely. A few minutes later they stagger out again, bottoms first.

*

1 June

The dry spell continues. It is only before sunrise that there is any freshness in the air.

At dawn I said, 'Day, you will not begin without me.' I was up with the whistling-thrush at five. The cicadas were tuning up, the crickets were already in full cry, and the whistling-thrush was calling most sweetly. As none of these songsters could be seen, it was as though the forest itself was singing.

Feeling the dawn wind stir, I was happy that I had met the day at its very beginning.

When the sun came up, the day became sultry and oppressive. I had to walk two miles to Ban Suman and back. There was no shade anywhere along the road. But we are equipped with legs for the purpose of walking. As more and more people grow dependent on their cars, a new species of humans will evolve. Around the turn of the twenty-second century, I can see legless humans being born. By then, of course, there will be flying wheelchairs.

A pall of dust hangs over the mountain.

Someone asked Sir E if he could shoot a bird on his land at Ramgarh. The man wanted the bird for dissection in a biology lab. Sir E refused.

'It's in the interests of science,' protested the man. 'Do you think a bird is better than a human?'

'Infinitely,' said Sir E. 'Infinitely better.'

He goes down today to pay his farm-hands. He will return in a few days unless it gets cooler in Dehra. He complains of being very bored up here, for he can't get about, and in Dehra he has his Hillman. 'I'm *rotting* with boredom,' he says.

Vinod, I hear, is laid low with a fever—the result of a day's hard work. He is now in retirement for the rest of the season.

*

Walked five miles down the Tehri road to Suakholi, where I rested in a small teashop, a loose stone structure with a tin roof held down by stones. It serves the bus passengers, mule drivers, milkmen and others who use this road.

I find a couple of mules tethered to a pine tree. The mule drivers, handsome men in tattered clothes, sit on a bench in the shade of the tree, drinking tea from brass tumblers. The shopkeeper, a man of indeterminate age—the cold dry winds from the mountain passes having crinkled his face like a walnut—greets me enthusiastically, as he always does. He even produces a chair, which looks like a survivor from the Savoy's 1890 ballroom. Fortunately the Mussoorie antique-dealers haven't seen it, or it would have been carried away long ago. In any case, the stuffing has come out of the seat. The shopkeeper apologizes for its condition: 'The rats were nesting in it.' And then, to reassure me: 'But they have gone now.'

Unlike the shopkeeper, the mule drivers have somewhere to go and something to deliver: sacks of potatoes. From Jaunpur to Jaunsar, the potato is probably the crop best suited to these stony, terraced fields. Oddly enough, it was introduced to the Himalayas by two Irishmen, Captain Young of Dehra and Mussoorie and Captain Kennedy of Simla, in the 1820s. The slopes of Young's house, 'Mullingar', were known as his Potato Farm. Looking up old books, I was surprised to learn that the potato wasn't known in India before the nineteenth century, and now it's an essential part of our diet in most parts of the country.

As the mule drivers lead their pack animals away, along the dusty road to Landour bazaar, I follow at a distance, singing 'Mule Train' in my best Nelson Eddy manner.*

*

A thunderstorm, followed by strong winds, brought down the temperature. That was yesterday. And today, June, it is cloudy, cool, drizzling a little, almost monsoon weather; but it is still too early for the real monsoon.

The birds are enjoying the cool weather. The green-backed tits cool their bottoms in the rainwater pool. A king-crow flashes past, winging through the air like an arrow. On the wing, it snaps up a hovering dragonfly. The mynahs fetch crow-feathers to line their nest in the eaves of the house. I am lying so still on the window-seat that a tit alights on the sill within a few inches of my head. It snaps up a small dead moth before flying away.

Sir E is back. He found it too hot in the valley. Even up here he has given up wearing a necktie. I'll have him wearing a kurta and pyjamas before long; the only sensible dress in summer.

At dusk I sit at the window and watch the trees and listen to the wind as it makes light conversation in the leafy tops of the maples. A large bat flits in and out of the trees. The sky is

---

*Not Nelson's song originally, but he sang it better than anyone else.

just light enough to enable me to see the bat and the outlines of the taller trees. Up on Landour hill, the lights are just beginning to come on. It is deliciously cool, eight o'clock, a perfect summer's evening. Prem is singing to himself in the kitchen. His wife and sister are chattering beneath the walnut tree. Down the hill, a *kakar* is barking, alarmed perhaps by the presence of a leopard. All the birds have gone to sleep for the night. Even the cicadas are strangely silent. The wind grows stronger and the tall maples bow before it: the maple moves its slender branches slowly from side to side, the oak moves its branches up and down. It is darker now; more lights on Landour. The cry of the barking-deer has grown fainter, more distant, and now I hear a cricket singing in the bushes. The stars are out, the wind grows chilly, it is time to close the window.

*

Bijju is very much an outdoor boy, even when he isn't grazing cows. He isn't very strong in the chest, but his legs are sturdy; he was having no difficulty in scaling the high retaining wall. He grinned down at me. He is rather like the whistling-thrush—absent for days, then unexpectedly reappearing in the forest or on the hillside. Bijju sings too, although his voice is more vigorous than melodic. And that reminds me of the story of the whistling-thrush. The bird was once a village boy who tried very hard to play the flute in the same style as the god Krishna. When the god heard his favourite melody being plagiarized, he was furious and turned the unfortunate boy into a bird. The whistling-thrush still tries to copy the divine melody, but somehow it always breaks off right in the middle of a stanza. There ought to be a moral here, especially in a land full of plagiarists. Or to be fair, I should say film-land . . . .

*

The Whistler. This is my name for the youth who labours part-time in the school. He is something of a character—scatter-brained, carefree, easygoing. He is always whistling—loudly and quite tunefully (this time a bird turned into a boy?)—so that you know when he's coming round a bend or through the trees, and even when it's dark you know who it is. He's usually out quite late, because he spends all his money at the pictures. He has three sisters, and they and the mother are all working as maids or ayahs, and as they are quite indulgent to him (the only brother) he doesn't have to work too hard. His shoes are always torn, even though his clothes look new.

He has a reputation for being a waster, but he returned the few rupees he borrowed from me last month. I suppose a youth who is always singing and whistling on the roads gives everyone the impression that he has nothing to do from morn till night, unlike that jolly miller of Dee who worked *and* sang the whole day through. (I know one man who forbids his children from singing in the home.)

But back to the Whistler, he is really quite enterprising. The other day he asked me for one of my books, and as I knew he hadn't squandered too many years in school, I gave him an easy Hindi translation of one of my children's books. But it was the paper he valued, not the words. He flogged it to the bania's small son, who took it apart and converted the large pages into envelopes, which were then used for selling gram and peanuts. In India it doesn't take long for anything to be recycled. On the way home, I saw a couple of customers throwing their empty packets away, and these were promptly consumed by a stray cow. There went my beautiful story!

Is there a lesson to be learnt from this? Yes. Don't give away complimentaries.

*

It rained all night, and the morning is cool and fresh. Parrots are on the wing. I feel like tap-dancing like Gene Kelly, but you can't tap dance on a hillside, you'd break an ankle. Only the roads (and not all of them) are suitable for a song-and-dance act, and no doubt the Whistler will oblige before long. At forty, I must refrain from being too frisky and boyish. But I'll do a reel in the garden when no one is looking.

*

24 June

The first day of monsoon mist. And it's strange how all the birds fall silent as the mist comes climbing up the hill. Perhaps that's what makes the mist so melancholy; not only does it conceal the hills, it blankets them in silence too. Only an hour ago the trees were ringing with birdsong. And now the forest is deathly still, as though it were midnight.

Through the mist Bijju is calling to his sister. I can hear him running about on the hillside but I cannot see him.

Feeling sorry for Sir E (or maybe for myself), I walked over to see him. The door was closed, so I looked in at the French window (nothing could be more *English* than a French window, and no Agatha Christie mystery would be complete without one), I saw him sleeping in his chair with his chin on his chest. There was no dagger sticking out of his back, only a bit of stuffing from his old coat. My footsteps on the gravel woke him, and he got up and opened the door for me. He said he felt a bit tipsy; had taken his usual peg, but thought the quality of whisky varied from bottle to bottle, and wished he could lay his hands on a bottle of Scotch or even Irish. He could only offer me an Uttar Pradesh brand. I said I'd given up drinking, and this pleased him because in truth he hates anyone drinking his whisky; said he might give it up himself, it 'cost too damn much'! I told him it would be unwise to give up drinking at this stage of his life. As he had reached the age of eighty-six on two pegs a day, he was obviously thriving on it. Giving it up now would only play havoc with the orderly working of his system. I'd given it up in order to help an alcoholic friend abstain, and also because I wanted to give up *something*, and strong drink seemed the easiest thing to do without.

*

A cicada starts up in the tree nearest my window-seat. What has he been doing all these weeks, and why does he choose this particular moment and this particular evening to play the fiddle so loudly? The cicadas are late this year, the monsoon has been late. But soon the forest will be ringing with the sound of the cicadas—an orchestra constantly tuning up but never quite getting into tune—and the sound of the birds will be pushed into the background.

Outside the front door I found an elegant young praying-mantis reclining on a leaf of the honeysuckle creeper. I·say young because he hadn't grown to his full size, and was that very tender pale green which is the colour of a young mantis. They are light brown to begin with, like dry twigs, but as they grow older and the monsoon foliage becomes greener, they too change, and by mid-August they are dark green.

As though to make up for lost time, the monsoon rains are now here with a vengeance. It has been pouring all day, and already the roof is leaking. But nothing dampens Prem's spirits. He is still singing love songs in the kitchen.

*

Kailash, whom I have known for a couple of weeks, asks me for twenty-five rupees.

'What do you need it for?' I ask.

'It's for my Sanskrit teacher,' he says. 'I have failed in Sanskrit but if I give the teacher twenty-five rupees he'll alter my marks. You see, I've passed in all the other subjects, but if I fail in Sanskrit I'll fail the entire exam and remain a pre-Inter student for another year.'

I took a little time to digest this information and ponder on the pitfalls of the examination system.

'He must be failing a lot of boys,' I said. 'Twenty-five rupees each! Are there many others?'

'Some. But he dare not fail the good ones. They can ask for a re-check. It's the borderline cases like me who give him a chance to make money.'

This placed me in a quandary. Should I yield to the evils of the examination system and provide the money for pass-marks? Or should I adopt a high moral stance and allow the boy to fail?

Whatever the evils of the exam system, they are not the fault of the student. And either way he isn't going to turn into a great Sanskrit scholar. So why be a hypocrite? I gave him the money.

Kailash slogs in his uncle's orchard all morning, gets a

mid-day meal (no breakfast), and hasn't any shoes. And yet his uncle, a member of one of Garhwal's well-known upper caste families, is a wealthy man.

Kailash tells me he will return to his village once he knows his result. According to him his uncle is such a miser that at mealtimes he pauses before each mouthful, wondering: 'Ought I to eat it? Or should I keep it for tomorrow?'

*

I am visited by another kind of student, a small girl from one of the private schools. Her mother has brought her to me for my autograph.

'She studies your book in Class 6,' I was informed.

'And what book is that?' I asked the little girl.

'Tom Sawyer,' she replied promptly. So I signed for Mark Twain.

*

When a small storeroom collapsed during the last heavy rains, I was forced to rescue a couple of old packing-cases that had been left there for three or four years—since my arrival here, in fact. The contents were well-soaked and most of it had to be thrown away—old manuscripts that had been obliterated, negatives that had got stuck together, gramophone records that had taken on strange shapes (dear 'Ink Spots', how will I ever listen to you again?*) . . . . Unlike most writers, I have no compunction about throwing away work that hasn't quite come off, and I am sure there are a few critics who would prefer that I throw away the lot! Sentimental rubbish, no doubt. Well, we can't please everyone; and we can't preserve everything either. Time and the elements will take their toll.

But a couple of old diaries, kept in exercise books almost twenty years ago, had managed to survive the rain, and I put them out in the sun to dry, and then, almost unwillingly, started browsing through them. It was instructive, and

---

* This was before the advent of audiotapes

sometimes a little disconcerting, to discover the sort of person I had been in my twenties. In some ways, no different from what I am today. In other ways, radically different. A diary is a useful tool for self-examination, particularly if both diary and diarist are still around after some years.

One particular entry caught my eye, and I reproduce it here without any alteration, because it represented my credo as a young writer, and it set me wondering if I had lived up to my own expectations. (Nobody else had any expectations of me!)

The entry was made on 19 January 1958, when I was living on my own in Dehradun:

> The things I do best are those things I do on my own, alone, of my own accord, without the advice or approval of others. Once I start doing what other people tell me to do, both my character and creativity take a dip. It is when I strike out on my own that I succeed best.

> There was a time when I was much younger and poorer than I am now. I had been over a year in Jersey, in the Channel Islands; I was unhappy, and the atmosphere in which I was writing was one of discouragement and disapproval. And that was why I wrote so well—because I was defiant! That was why I finished the only book I have finished so far. I had to prove to myself that I could do it.

> One night I was walking alone along the beach. There was a strong wind blowing, dashing the salt spray in my face, and the sea was crashing against the St. Helier rocks. I told myself: I will go to London; I will take up a job; I will finish my book; I will find a publisher; I will save money and I will return to India, because I can be happier there than here.

> And that was just what I did.
> I had guts then.
> What's more, I had an end in view.

23

The writing itself is not enough for me. Success and money are not enough. I had a little of both recently,* but they did not help me to do anything wonderful. I must have something to write for, just as I must have something to live for. And that's something I have yet to find.

There was more in that vein, but I give this excerpt as an example of a young man's determination to be a writer in what were then adverse circumstances. Thirty-five years later, I'm still trying.

*

27 June

The rains have heralded the arrival of some seasonal visitors—a leopard; and several thousand leeches.

Yesterday afternoon the leopard lifted a dog from near the servants' quarters below the school. In the evening it attacked one of Bijju's cows but fled at the approach of Bijju's mother, who came screaming imprecations.

As for the leeches, I shall soon get used to a little blood-letting every day. Bijju's mother sat down in the shrubbery to relieve herself, and later discovered two fat black leeches feeding on her fair round bottom. I told her she could use one of the spare bathrooms downstairs. But she prefers the wide open spaces.

Other new arrivals are the scarlet minivets (the females are yellow), flitting silently among the leaves like brilliant jewels. No matter how leafy the trees, these brightly coloured birds cannot conceal themselves, although, by remaining absolutely silent, they sometimes contrive to go unnoticed. Along come a pair of drongos, unnecessarily aggressive, chasing the minivets away.

A tree-creeper moves rapidly up the trunk of the oak tree, snapping up insects all the way. Now that the rains are here, there is no dearth of food for the insectivorous birds.

In spite of there being water in several places, the whistling-

---

* When *The Room on the Roof* was published (1956).

thrush still comes to my pool. He, at least, is a permanent resident.

*

Kailash has a round, cheerful face, only slightly marred by a swivel eye. His hair comes down over his forehead, hiding a deep scar. He is short, but quite compact and energetic. He chatters a good deal but in a general sort of way, and a response isn't obligatory.

It's quite possible that he will go away as soon as he gets his exam results. He's fed up with being the Cinderfella of his uncle's house. He tells of how his miserly uncle went to see a rather permissive film, and was very shocked and wanted to walk out, but couldn't bear the thought of losing his ticket money; so he sat through the film with his eyes closed.

*

Sir E departed for Dehra with his large retinue of servants and their dependants, all of whom would have done justice to an eighteenth century nabob.

'I am at the mercy of my servants,' he told me the other day.

But he had placed himself at their mercy long ago, by setting himself up as a country squire surrounded by 'faithful retainers'—all of whom received generous salaries but little or no work. If he sold his white elephant of a farm, he'd be quite comfortable with one servant.

'I'll probably come up in September, after the rains,' he said. 'If I live that long . . . . I'm just living from day to day.'

'So am I,' I told him. 'It's the best way to live.'

*

A couple of days passed before Kailash came to see me. I was beginning to wonder if he'd come again. Apparently the teacher had at first proved elusive; but the deed was done, and Kailash passed with the marks he needed. Ironically, his uncle was so impressed that he is now urging the boy to remain with him and complete the Intermediate exam.

'I must write a story about your uncle,' I remark.

'Don't give him a story,' says Kailash. 'A short note will do.'

Now that Prem is preoccupied with his wife, and the house is at the mercy of uninvited visitors, I stay out most of the time, and these days Kailash is my only companion. Yesterday we took the Camel's Back Road, past the cemetery. He chatters away, and I can listen if I want to, or think of other things if I don't want to listen; apparently it makes no difference to him. He is a cheerful soul, with an infectious laugh. He walks with a slight swagger, or roll. He says he doesn't mind staying here now that he has me for a friend; that he can put up with two sour uncles as long as he knows I'm around. I suspect he's quite capable of pulling a fast one on his uncle; but all the same, I find myself liking him.

*

Moody. And when I'm moody I'm bad.

Prem says: 'It is easier to please God than it is to please you.'

'But God is easily pleased,' I respond. 'God makes absolutely no demands on us. We just imagine them.'

The eyes.

Prem's eyes have great gentleness in them.

His wife's eyes are round and mischievous and suggestive . . . .

Suggestive enough to invite the attention of a mischievous or malignant spirit.

At about two in the morning I am awakened by Prem's shouts, muffled by rain. Shouting back that I am on my way, for it is obviously an emergency, I leap out of bed, grab an umbrella, dash outside and then down the stairs to his room. His wife is sobbing in bed. Whatever had possessed her has now gone away, and the crying is due more to Prem's ministrations—he exorcizes the ghost by thumping her on the head—than to the 'possession' itself. But there is no doubt that she is subject to hallucinatory or subconscious actions. It is not simply a hysterical fit. She walks in her sleep, moves restlessly from door to window, holds conversations with an invisible presence, and resists all efforts to bring her back to reality.

When she comes out of the trance, she is quite normal.

This sort of thing is apparently quite common in the hills, where people believe it to be a ghost taking temporary possession of a human mind. It's happened to Prem's wife before, and it also happens to her brother, so it seems to run in families. It never happens to Prem, who deeply resents the interruption to his sleep.

I calm the girl and then make them bring their bedding upstairs. I give her a sleeping tablet and she is soon fast asleep.

During a lull in the rain, I hear a most hideous sound coming from the forest—a maniacal shrieking, followed by a mournful hooting. But Prem and his wife sleep through it all. The rain starts again, and the shrieking stops. Perhaps it's a hyaena. Perhaps something else.

*

A morning of bright sunshine, and the whistling-thrush welcomes it with a burst of song. Where do the birds shelter when it rains? How does that frail butterfly survive the battering of strong winds and heavy rain-drops? How do the snakes manage in their flooded holes?

I saw a bright green snake sunning itself on some rocks; no doubt waiting for its hole to dry out.

*

In my vagrant days, ten to fifteen years ago (long before the hippies made vagrancy a commonplace), I was a great frequenter of teashops, those dingy little shacks with a table and three chairs, a grimy tea-kettle, and a cracked gramophone. Teashops haven't changed much, and once again I find myself lingering in them, sometimes in company with Kailash, who, although he doesn't eat much, drinks a lot of tea.

One can sit all day in a teashop and watch the world go by. Amazing the number of people who actually do this! And not all of them unemployed. The teashop near the clock tower is ideal for this purpose. It is a busy part of the bazaar but the teashop, though small, is gloomy within, and one can loll about unseen, observing everyone who passes by a few feet away in the sunlit (or rain-spattered) street. The tea itself is indifferent, the buns are stale, the boiled eggs have been peppered too liberally. Kailash is unusually quiet, there is no one else in the shop. People who would stop me in the road pass by without glancing into the murky interior. This is the ideal place; not as noble as my window opening into the trees, but familiar, reminiscent of days gone by in Dehra, when cares sat lightly upon me simply because I did not care at all. And now perhaps I have begun to care too much.

I gave Bijju a cake. He licked all the icing off it, only then did he eat the rest.

*

It was a dark windy corner in Landour bazaar, but I always found the old man there, hunched up over the charcoal fire on which he roasted his peanuts. He'd been there for as long as I could remember, and he could be seen at almost any hour of the day or night. Summer or winter, he stayed close to his fire.

He was probably quite tall, but we never saw him standing up. One judged his height from his long, loose limbs. He was very thin, and the high cheekbones added to the tautness of his tightly stretched skin.

His peanuts were always fresh, crisp and hot. They were popular with the small boys who had a few paise to spend on their way to and from school, and with the patrons of the cinemas, many of whom made straight for the windy corner during intervals or when the show was over. On cold winter evenings, or misty monsoon days, there was always a demand for the old man's peanuts.

No one knew his name. No one had ever thought of asking him for it. One just took him for granted. He was as fixed a landmark as the clock tower or the old cherry tree that grew crookedly from the hillside. The tree was always being lopped; the clock often stopped. The peanut vendor seemed less perishable than the tree, more dependable than the clock.

He had no family, but in a way all the world was his family, because he was in continuous contact with people. And yet he was a remote sort of being; always polite, even to children, but never familiar. There is a distinction to be made between aloneness and loneliness. The peanut vendor was seldom alone; but he must have been lonely.

Summer nights he rolled himself up in a thin blanket and slept on the ground, beside the dying embers of his fire. During the winter, he waited until the last show was over, before retiring to the rickshaw-coolies' shed where there was some protection from the biting wind.

Did he enjoy being alive? I wonder now. He was not a joyful person; but then, neither was he miserable. I should think he was a genuine stoic, one of those who do not attach overmuch importance to themselves, who are emotionally uninvolved, content with their limitations, their dark corners. I wanted to get to know the old man better, to sound him out on the immense questions involved in roasting peanuts all his life; but it's too late now. The last time I visited the bazaar the dark corner was deserted; the old man had vanished; the coolies had carried him down to the cremation ground.

'He died in his sleep,' said the teashop-owner. 'He was very old.'

Very old. Sufficient reason to die.

But that corner is very empty, very dark, and whenever I pass it I am haunted by visions of the old peanut vendor, troubled by the questions I failed to ask; and I wonder if he was really as indifferent to life as he appeared to be.

*

Prem brought his wife some of her favourite mangoes. This afternoon he took her into my room so that she could listen to the radio. They both fell asleep at opposite ends of the bed; are still asleep as I write this in the next room, at my window. If I curled up a little, I could fall asleep here on the window-seat. Nothing would induce me to disturb those innocents; they look far too blissful in their slumbers.

*

Kailash and I are caught in a storm and it's by far the worst storm of the year. To make matters worse, there is absolutely no shelter for a mile along the main road from the town. It was fierce, lashing rain, quite cold, whipping along on the wind from all angles. The road was soon a torrent of muddy water, as earth and stones came rushing down the hillsides. Our one umbrella was useless and was very nearly blown away. The cardboard carton in which we were carrying vegetables was soon reduced to pulp. We broke into a run, although we could hardly see our way. There were blinding flashes of lightning— is an umbrella a good or a bad conductor of electricity? Kailash sees humour in these situations and was in peals of laughter all the way home, even when we slid into a ditch.

He takes my hand and holds it between his hands. He is happy. He has got his self-confidence back, and can now deal with his uncles and Sanskrit teachers.

In the morning I work on a story. There is a dove cooing in the garden. Now it is very quiet, the only sound is the distant tapping of a woodpecker. The trees are muffled in ferns and creepers. It is mid-monsoon.

Kailash, his hair falling in an untidy mop across his forehead, drags me out of the house and over the wet green grass on the hillside. I protest that I do not like leeches, so we make for the high rocks. He laughs, talks, chuckles, and when he grins his large front teeth make him look like a 1940s' Mickey Rooney. When he looks sullen (this happens when he talks about his uncle), he looks Brando-ish. He has the gift of being able to convey his effervescence to me. Am I, at thirty-eight, too old to be gambolling about on the hill slopes like a young colt? (Am I, sobering thought, going to be a character of enforced youthfulness like the man on the boat in *Death in Venice*? Well, better that than the Gissing hero of *New Grub Street* who's old at forty.) If I am fit enough to gambol, than I must gambol. If I can still climb a tree, then I must climb trees, instead of just watching them from my window. I was in such high spirits yesterday that I kept playing the clown, and I haven't done this in years. To walk in the rain was fun, and to get wet was fun, and to fall down was fun, and to get hurt was fun.

30

'Will it last?' asks Kailash. 'This feeling of love between us?'
'*This* won't last. Not in this way. But if something *like* it lasts,
we should be happy.'

*

Prem is happy, laughing, giggling all the time. Sometimes it is
a little annoying for me, because he is obviously unaware of
what is happening around him—such as the fact that part of
the roof blew away in the storm—but I am a good Taoist, I say
nothing, I wait for the right moment! Besides, it's a crime to
interfere with anyone's happiness.

*

Prem notices the roof is missing and scolds his wife for seeing
too many pictures. 'She's seen ten pictures in two months.
More than she'd seen in her whole life, before coming here.'
She pulls a face. Says Prem: 'My grandfather will be here any
day to take her home.'
'Then she can see pictures with your grandfather,' I venture.
'While we repair the roof.'
'I wouldn't go anywhere with that old man,' she says.
'Don't speak like that of my grandfather. Do you want a
beating? Look at Binya'—we all look at Binya, who is perched
very prettily on the wall—'she hasn't seen more than two
pictures in her life!'
'I'll take her to the pictures,' I offer.
Binya gives me a radiant smile. She'd love to go to the
pictures, but her mother won't allow it.
Prem relents and takes his wife to the pictures.
Binya's mother has a bad attack of hiccups. Serves her right,
for stealing my walnuts and not letting me take Binya to the
pictures.
In the evening I find Prem teaching his wife the alphabet,
using the kitchen door as a blackboard. It is covered with chalk
marks. Love is teaching your wife to read and write!

*

These entries were made in 1973, twenty years ago.

The following year I did not keep a journal, but these are some of the things that happened:

Sir E had a stroke and, like a stranded whale, finally heaved his last breath. According to his wishes, he was cremated on his farm near Dehra.

To Prem and Chandra was born a son, Rakesh, who immediately stole my heart—and gave me many a sleepless night, for as a baby he cried lustily.

Kailash went into the army and disappeared from my life, as well as from his uncle's.

Bijju and Binya were to remain a part of the hillside for several years.

Voting at Barlowganj

I AM STANDING under the deodars, waiting for a taxi. Devilal, one of the candidates in the civic election, is offering free rides to all his supporters, to ensure that they get to the polls in time. I have assured him that I prefer walking but he does not believe me; he fears that I will settle down with a bottle of beer rather than walk the two miles to the Barlowganj polling station to cast my vote. He has gone to the expense of engaging a taxi for the day just to make certain of lingerers like me. He assures me that he is not using unfair means—most of the other candidates are doing the same thing.

It is a cloudy day, promising rain, so I decide I will wait for the taxi. It has been plying since six a.m., and now it is ten o'clock. It will continue plying up and down the hill till four p.m. and by that time it will have cost Devilal over a hundred rupees.

Here it comes. The driver—like most of our taxi-drivers, a Sikh—sees me standing at the gate, screeches to a sudden stop, and opens the door. I am about to get in when I notice that the windscreen carries a sticker displaying the Congress symbol of the cow and calf. Devilal is an Independent, and has adopted a cock-bird as his symbol.

'Is this Devilal's taxi?' I ask.

'No, it's the Congress taxi,' says the driver.

'I'm sorry,' I say. 'I don't know the Congress candidate.'

'That's all right,' he says agreeably; he isn't a local man and has no interest in the outcome of the election. 'Devilal's taxi will be along any minute now.'

He moves off, looking for the Congress voters on whose behalf he has been engaged. I am glad that the candidates have had to adopt different symbols; it has saved me the embarrassment of turning up in a Congress taxi, only to vote for an Independent. But the real reason for using symbols is to help illiterate voters know whom they are voting for when it comes to putting their papers in the ballot-box. All through the hill-station's mini-election campaign, posters have been displaying candidates' symbols—a car, a radio, a cock-bird, a tiger, a lamp—and the narrow, winding roads resound to the cries of children who are paid to shout, 'Vote for the Radio!' or 'Vote for the Cock!'

Presently my taxi arrives. It is already full, having picked up others on the way, and I have to squeeze in at the back with a stout *lalain* and her bony husband, the local ration-shop owner. Sitting up front, near the driver, is Vinod, a poor, ragged, quite happy-go-lucky youth, who contrives to turn up wherever I happen to be, and frequently involves himself in my activities. He gives me a namaste and a wide grin.

'What are you doing here?' I ask him.

'Same as you, Bond sahib. Voting. Maybe Devilal will give me a job if he wins.'

'But you already have a job. I thought you were the games-boy at the school.'

'That was last month, Bond sahib.'

'They kicked you out?'

'They asked me to leave.'

The taxi gathers speed as it moves smoothly down the winding hill road. The driver is in a hurry; the more trips he makes the more money he collects. We swerve round sharp corners, and every time the *lalain's* chubby hands, covered with heavy bangles and rings, clutch at me for support. She and her husband are voting for Devilal because they belong to the same caste; Vinod is voting for him in the hope of getting a job; I am voting for him because I like the man. I find him simple, courteous and ready to listen to complaints about drains, street-lighting and wrongly-assessed taxes. He even tries to do something about these things. He is a tall, cadaverous man, with paan-stained teeth; no Nixon, Heath or Indira Gandhi; but he knows that Barlowganj folk care little for appearances.

Barlowganj is a small ward (one of four in the hill-station of

Mussoorie); it has about one thousand voters. An election campaign has, therefore, to be conducted on a person-to-person basis. There is no point in haranguing a crowd at a street corner; it would be a very small crowd. The only way to canvass support is to visit each voter's house and plead one's cause personally. This means making a lot of promises with a perfectly straight face.

The bazaar and village of Barlowganj crouch in a vale on the way down the mountain to Dehra. The houses on either side of the road are nearly all English-looking most of them built before the turn of the century. The bazaar is Indian, charming and quite prosperous: tailors sit cross-legged before their sewing machines, turning out blazers and tight trousers for the well-to-do students who attend the many public schools that still thrive here; *halwais*—pot-bellied sweet vendors—spend all day sitting on their haunches in front of giant frying-pans; and coolies carry huge loads of timber or cement or grain up the steep hill paths.

Who was Barlow, and how did the village get his name? A search through old guides and gazetteers has given me no clue. Perhaps he was a revenue superintendent or a surveyor, who came striding up from the plains in the 1830s to build a hunting-lodge in this pleasantly wooded vale. That was how most hill-stations began. The police station, the little Church of the Resurrection, and the ruined brewery were among the earliest buildings in Barlowganj.

The brewery is a mound of rubble, but the road that came into existence to serve the needs of the old Crown Brewery is the one that now serves our taxi. Buckle and Co.'s 'Bullock Train' was the chief means of transport in the old days. Mr Bohle, one of the pioneers of brewing in India, started the 'Old Brewery' at Mussoorie in 1830. Two years later he got into trouble with the authorities for supplying beer to soldiers without permission; he had to move elsewhere.

But the great days of the brewery business really began in 1876, when everyone suddenly acclaimed a much-improved brew. The source was traced to Vat 42 in Whymper's Crown Brewery (the one whose ruins we are now passing), and the beer was retasted and retested until the diminishing level of the barrel revealed the perfectly brewed remains of a soldier who had been reported missing some months previously. He had evidently fallen into the vat and been drowned and, unknown to himself, had given the Barlowganj beer trade a real fillip. Apocryphal though this story may sound, I have it on the authority of the owner of the now defunct *Mafasalite Press* who, in a short account of Mussoorie, wrote that 'meat was thereafter recognized as the missing component and was scrupulously added till more modern, and less cannibalistic, means were discovered to satiate the froth-blower.'

Recently, confirmation came from an old India hand now living in London. He wrote to me reminiscing of early days in the hill-station and had this to say:

> Uncle Georgie Forster was working for the Crown Brewery when a coolie fell in. Coolies were employed to remove scum etc. from the vats. They walked along planks suspended over the vats. Poor devil must have slipped and fallen in. Uncle often told us about the incident and there was no doubt that the beer tasted very good.

What with soldiers and coolies falling into the vats with seeming regularity, one wonders whether there may have been more to these accidents than met the eye. I have a nagging suspicion that Whymper and Buckle may have been the Burke and Hare of Mussoorie's beer industry.

But no beer is made in Mussoorie today, and Devilal probably regrets the passing of the breweries as much as I do. Only the walls of the breweries remain, and these are several feet thick. The roofs and girders must have been removed for use in other buildings. Moss and sorrel grow in the old walls, and wild cats live in dark corners protected from rain and wind.

We have taken the sharpest curves and steepest gradients, and now our taxi moves smoothly along a fairly level road which might pass for a country lane in England were it not for the clumps of bamboo on either side.

A mist has come up the valley to settle over Barlowganj, and out of the mist looms an imposing mansion, Sikander Hall, which is still owned and occupied by Skinners, descendants of Colonel James Skinner who raised a body of Irregular Horse for the Marathas. This was absorbed by the East India Company's forces in 1803. The Cavalry regiment is still known as Skinners Horse, but of course it is a tank regiment now. Skinner's troops called him 'Sikander' (a corruption of both Skinner and Alexander), and that is the name his property bears. The Skinners who live here now have, quite sensibly, gone in for keeping pigs and poultry.

The next house belongs to the Raja of K but he is unable to maintain it on his diminishing privy-purse, and it has been rented out as an ashram for members of a saffron-robed sect who would rather meditate in the hills than in the plains. There was a time when it was only the sahibs and rajas who could afford to spend the entire 'season' in Mussoorie. The new rich are the industrialists and maharishis. The coolies and rickshaw-pullers are no better off than when I was a boy in Mussoorie. They still carry or pull the same heavy loads, for the same pittance, and seldom attain the age of forty. Only their clientele has changed.

One more gate, and here is Colonel Powell in his khaki bush-shirt and trousers, a uniform that never varies with the seasons. He is an old shikari; once wrote a book called *The Call of the Tiger*. He is too old for hunting now, but likes to yarn with me when we meet on the road. His wife has gone home to England, but he does not want to leave India.

'It's the mountains,' he was telling me the other day. 'Once the mountains are in your blood, there is no escape. You have to come back again and again. I don't think I'd like to die anywhere else.'

Today there is no time to stop and chat. The taxi-driver, with a vigorous blowing of his horn, takes the car round the last bend, and then through the village and narrow bazaar of Barlowganj, stopping about a hundred yards from the polling stations.

There is a festive air about Barlowganj today, I have never

37

seen so many people in the bazaar. Bunting, in the form of rival posters and leaflets, is strung across the street. The teashops are doing a roaring trade. There is much last-minute canvassing, and I have to run the gamut of various candidates and their agents. For the first time I learn the names of some of the candidates. In all, seven men are competing for this seat.

A schoolboy, smartly dressed and speaking English, is the first to accost me. He says: 'Don't vote for Devilal, sir. He's a big crook. Vote for Jatinder! See, sir, that's his symbol—the bow and arrow.'

'I shall certainly think about the bow and arrow,' I tell him politely.

Another agent, a man, approaches, and says, 'I hope you are going to vote for the Congress candidate.'

'I don't know anything about him,' I say.

'That doesn't matter. It's the party you are voting for. Don't forget it's Mrs Gandhi's party.'

Meanwhile, one of Devilal's lieutenants has been keeping a close watch on both Vinod and me, to make sure that we are not seduced by rival propaganda. I give the man a reassuring smile and stride purposefully towards the polling station, which has been set up in the municipal schoolhouse. Policemen stand at the entrance, to make sure that no one approaches the voters once they have entered the precincts.

I join the patient queue of voters. Everyone is in good humour, and there is no breaking of the line; these are not film stars we have come to see. Vinod is in another line, and grins proudly at me across the passageway. This is the one day in his life on which he has been made to feel really important. And he *is*. In a small constituency like Barlowganj every vote counts.

Most of my fellow-voters are poor people. Local issues mean something to them, affect their daily living. The more affluent can buy their way out of trouble, can pay for small conveniences; few of them bother to come to the polls. But for the 'common' man'—the shopkeeper, clerk, teacher, domestic servant, milkman, mule-driver—this is a big day. The man he is voting for has promised him something, and the voter means to take the successful candidate up on his promise. Not for another five years will the same fuss be made over the local cobblers, tailors and laundrymen. Their votes are indeed precious.

And now it is my turn to vote. I confirm my name, address and roll-number. I am down on the list as 'Rusking Bound', but I let it pass: I might forfeit my right to vote if I raise any objection at this stage! A dab of marking-ink is placed on my forefinger—this is so that I do not come round a second time—and I am given a paper displaying the names and symbols of all the candidates. I am then directed to the privacy of a small booth, where I place the official rubber-stamp against Devilal's name. This done, I fold the paper in four and slip it into the ballot-box.

All has gone smoothly. Vinod is waiting for me outside. So is Devilal.

'Did you vote for me?' asks Devilal.

It is my eyes that he is looking at, not my lips, when I reply in the affirmative. He is a shrewd man, with many years' experience in seeing through bluff. He is pleased with my reply, beams at me, and directs me to the waiting taxi.

Vinod and I get in together, and soon we are on the road again, being driven swiftly homewards up the winding hill road.

Vinod is looking pleased with himself; rather smug, in fact.

'You did vote for Devilal?' I ask him. 'The symbol of the cock-bird?'

He shakes his head, keeping his eyes on the road. 'No, the cow,' he says.

'You ass!' I exclaim. 'Devilal's symbol was the cock, not the cow!'

'I know,' he says, 'but I like the cow better.'

I subside into silence. It is a good thing no one else in the taxi has been paying any attention to our conversation. It would be a pity to see Vinod turned out of Devilal's taxi and made to walk the remaining mile to the top of the hill. After all, it will be another five years before he gets another free taxi-ride.

(In spite of Vinod's defection, Devilal won.)

1974

Miss Bun and Others

1 *March 1975*

BEER IN THE sun. High in the spruce tree the barbet calls, heralding summer. A few puffy clouds drift lazily over the mountains. Is this the great escape?

I could sit here all day, soaking up beer and sunshine, but at *some* time during the day I must wipe the dust from my typewriter and produce something readable. There's only Rs 800 in the bank, book sales are falling off, and magazines are turning away from fiction.

Prem spoils me, gives me rice and kofta curry for lunch, which means that I sleep till four when Miss Bun arrives with patties and samosas.

Miss Bun is the baker's daughter.

Of course that's not her real name. Her real name is very long and beautiful, but I won't give it here for obvious reasons and also because her brother is big and ugly.

I am seeing Miss Bun after two months. She's been with relatives in Bareilly.

She sits at the foot of my bed, absolutely radiant. Her raven-black hair lies loose on her shoulders; her eyelashes have been trimmed and blackened; so have her eyes, with *kajal*. Her eyes, so large and innocent—and calculating!

There are pretty glass bangles on her wrists and she wears a pair of new slippers. Her kameez is new, too; green silk, with gold-embroidered sleeves.

'You must have a rich lover,' I remark, taking her hand and gently pulling her toward me. 'Who gave you all this finery?'

'You did. Don't you remember? Before I went away, you gave me a hundred rupees.'

'That was for the train and bus fares. I thought.'

'Oh, my uncle paid the fares. So I bought myself these things. Are they nice?'

'Very pretty. And so are you. If you were ten years older, and I was ten years younger, we'd make a good pair. But, I'd have been broke long before this!'

She giggles and drops a paper-bag full of samosas on the bedside table. I hate samosas and patties, but I keep ordering them because it gives Miss Bun a pretext for visiting me. It's all in the way of helping the bakery get by. When she goes, I give the lot to Bijju and Binya or whoever might be passing.

'You've been away a long time,' I complain. 'What if I'd got married while you were away?'

'Then you'd stop ordering samosas.'

'Or get them from that old man Bashir, who makes much better ones, and cheaper!'

She drops her head on my shoulder. Her hair is heavily scented with jasmine hair-oil, and I nearly pass out. They should use it instead of anaesthesia.

'You smell very nice,' I lie. 'Do I get a kiss?'

She gives me a long kiss, as though to make up for her long absence. Her kisses always have a nice wholesome flavour, as you would expect from someone who lives in a bakery.

'That was an expensive kiss.'

'I want to buy some face-cream.'

'You don't need face-cream. Your complexion is perfect. It must be the good quality flour you use in the bakery.'

'I don't put flour on my face. Anyway, I want the cream for my elder sister. She has pock-marks.

I surrender and give her two fives, quickly putting away my wallet.

'And when will you pay for the samosas?'

'Next week.'

'I'll bring you something nice next week,' she says, pausing in the doorway.

'Well, thanks, I was getting tired of samosas.'

She was gone in a twinkling.

I'll say this for Miss Bun: she doesn't trouble to hide her intentions.

41

4 March

My policeman calls on me this morning. Ghanshyam, the constable attached to the Barlowganj outpost.

He is not very tall for a policeman, and he has a round, cheerful countenance, which is unusual in his profession. He looks smart in his uniform. Most constables prefer to hang around in their pyjamas most of the time.

Nothing alarming about Ghanshyam's visit. He comes to see me about once a week, and has been doing so ever since I spent a night in the police station last year.

It happened when I punched a Muzzaffarnagar businessman in the eye for bullying a rickshaw coolie. The fat slob very naturally lodged a complaint against me, and that same evening a sub-inspector called and asked me to accompany him to the *thana*. It was too late to arrange anything and in any case I had only been taken in for questioning, so I had to spend the night at the police post. The sub-inspector went home and left me in the charge of a constable. A wooden bench and a charpoy, were the only items of furniture in my 'cell', if you could call it that. The charpoy was meant for the night-duty constable, but he very generously offered it to me.

'But where will you sleep?' I asked.

'Oh, I don't feel like sleeping. Usually I go to the night show at the Picture Palace, but I suppose I'll have to stay here because of you.'

He looked rather sulky. Obviously I'd ruined his plans for the night.

'You don't have to stay because of me,' I said. 'I won't tell the SHO. You go to the Picture Palace, I'll look after the *thana*.'

He brightened up considerably, but still looked a bit doubtful.

'You can trust me,' I said encouragingly. 'My grandfather was a private soldier who became a Buddhist.'

'Then I can trust you as far as your grandfather.' He was quite cheerful now, and sent for two cups of tea from the shop across the road. It came gratis, of course. A little later he left me, and I settled down on the cot and slept fitfully. The constable came back during the early hours and went to sleep on the bench. Next morning I was allowed to go home. The

Muzzaffarnagar businessman had got into another fight and was lodged in the main *thana*. I did not hear about the matter again.

Ghanshyam, the constable, having struck up a friendship with me, was to visit me from time to time.

And here he is today, boots shining, teeth gleaming, cheeks almost glowing, far too charming a person to be a policeman.

'Hello, Ghanshyam-bhai,' I welcome him. 'Sit down and have some tea.'

'No, I can't stop for long,' he says, but sits down beside me on the veranda steps. 'Can you do me a favour?'

'Sure. What is it?'

'I'm fed up with Barlowganj. I want to get a transfer.'

'And how can I help you? I don't know any *netas* or bigwigs.'

'No, but our SP will be here next week, and he can have me transferred. Will you speak to him?'

'But why should he listen to me?'

'Well, you see, he has a weakness . . . .'

'We all have our weaknesses. Does your SP have a weakness similar to mine? Do we proceed to blackmail him?'

'Yes. You see, he writes poetry. And you are a *kavi*, a poet, aren't you?'

'At times,' I conceded. 'And I have to admit it's a weakness, especially as no one cares to read my poetry.'

'No one reads the SP's poetry, either. Although we have to listen to it sometimes. When he has finished reading out one of his poems, we salute and say *"Shabash!"'*

'A captive audience. I wish I had one.'

Ignoring my sarcasm, Ghanshyam continued: 'The trouble is, he can't get anyone to publish his poems. This makes him bad-tempered and unsympathetic to applications for transfer. Can you help?'

'I am not a publisher. I can only salute like the rest of you.'

'But you know publishers, don't you? If you can get some of his poems published, he'd be very grateful. To you. To me. To both of us!'

'You really are an optimist.'

'Just one or two poems. You see, I've already told him about you. How you spent all night in the lock-up writing verses. He thinks you are a famous writer. He's depending on me now. If the poems get published, he will give me a transfer. I'm sick of Barlowganj!' He gives me a hug and pinches me on the cheek. Before he can go any further, I say: 'Well, I'll do me best—' I was thinking of a little magazine published in Bhopal where most of my rejects found a home. 'For your sake, I'll try. But first I must see the poems.'

'You shall even see the SP,' he promised. 'I'll bring him here next week. You can give him a cup of tea.'

He got up, gave me a smart salute, and went up the path with a spring in his step. The sort of man who knows how to get his transfers and promotions in a perfectly honest manner.

7 March

It gets warmer day by day.

This morning I decided to sunbathe—quite modestly, of course. Retaining my old khaki shorts but removing all other clothing, I stretched out on a mattress in the garden. Almost immediately I was disturbed by the baker (Miss Bun's father for a change), who presented me with two loaves of bread and half a dozen chocolate pastries, ordered the previous day. Then Prem's small son, Raki, turned up, demanding a pastry, and I gave him two. He insisted on joining me on the mattress, where he proceeded to drop crumbs in my hair and on my chest. '*Good* morning, Mr Bond!' came the dulcet tones of Mrs Biggs, leaning over the gate. Forgetting that she was short-sighted, I jumped to my feet, and at the same time my shorts slipped down over my knees. As I grabbed for them, Mrs Biggs's effusiveness reached greater heights. 'Why, what a lovely *agapanthus* you've got!' she exclaimed, referring no doubt to the solitary lily in the garden. I must confess I blushed. Then, recovering myself, I returned her greeting, remarking on the freshness of the morning.

Mrs Biggs, at eighty, was a little deaf as well, and replied, 'I'm very well, thank you, Mr Bond. Is that a child you're carrying?'

'Yes, Prem's small son.'

'Prem is your son? I didn't know you had a family.'

At this point Raki decided to pluck the spectacles off Mrs Biggs's nose, and after I had recovered them for her, she beat a hasty retreat. Later, the Rev. Mr Biggs came over to borrow a book.

'Just light reading,' he said. 'I can't concentrate for long periods.'

He has become extremely absent-minded and forgetful; one of the drawbacks of living to an advanced age. During a funeral last year, at which he took the funeral service, he read out the service for Burial at Sea. It was raining heavily at the time, and no one seemed to notice.

Now he borrows two of my Ross Macdonalds—the same two he read last month. I refrain from pointing this out. If he has forgotten the books already, it won't matter if he reads them again.

Having spent the better part of his seventy-odd years in India, the Rev. Biggs has a lot of stories to tell, his favourite being the one about the crocodile he shot in Orissa when he was a young man. He'd pitched his tent on the banks of a river and gone to sleep on a camp-cot. During the night he felt his cot moving, and before he could gather his wits, the cot had moved swiftly through the opening of the tent and was rapidly making its way down to the river. Mr Biggs leapt for dry land while the cot, firmly wedged on the back of the crocodile, disappeared into the darkness.

Crocodiles, it seems, often bury themselves in the mud when they go to sleep, and Mr Biggs had pitched his tent and made his bed on top of a sleeping crocodile. Waking in the night, it had made for the nearest water.

Mr Biggs shot it the following morning—or so he would have us believe—the crocodile having reappeared on the river bank with the cot still attached to its back.

Now, having told me this story for the umpteenth time, Biggs says he really must be going, and, returning to the bookshelf, extracts Gibbons' *Decline and Fall of the Roman Empire*, having forgotten the Ross Macdonalds on a side-table.

'I must do some serious reading,' he says. 'These modern novels are so violent.'

'Lots of violence in *Decline and Fall*,' I remark.

'Ah, but it's history isn't it? Well, I must go now, Mr Macdonald. Mustn't waste your time.'

As he steps outside, he collides with Miss Bun, who drops samosas all over the veranda steps.

'Oh, dear, I'm so sorry,' he apologizes, and starts picking up the samosas, despite my attempts to prevent him from doing so. He then takes the paper-bag from Miss Bun and replaces the samosas.

'And who is this little girl?' he said benignly, patting Miss Bun on the head. 'One of your nieces?'

'That's right, sir. My favourite niece.'

'Well, I must not keep you. Service as usual, on Sunday.'

'Right, Mr Biggs.'

I have never been to a local church service, but why disillusion Rev. Biggs? I shall defend everyone's right to go to a place of worship provided they allow me the freedom to stay away.

Miss Bun is staring after Rev. Biggs as he crosses the road. Her mouth is slightly agape. 'What's the matter?' I ask.

'He's taken all the samosas!'

*

When I kiss Miss Bun, she bites my lip and draws blood.

'What was that for?' I complain.

'Just to make you angry.'

'But I don't like getting angry.'

'That's why.'

I get angry just to please her, and we take a tumble on the carpet.

11 March

Does anyone here make money? Apart, of course, from the traders, who tuck it all away . . . .

A young man turned up yesterday, selling geraniums. He

had a bag full of geraniums—cuttings and whole plants.

'All colours,' he told me confidently. 'Only one rupee a cutting.'

'I can buy them much cheaper at the government nursery.'

'But you would have to walk there, sir—six miles! I have brought these to your very doorstep. I will plant them for you, in your empty ghee tins, at no extra cost!'

'That's all right, you can give me a few. But what makes you sell geraniums?'

'I have nothing to eat, sir. I haven't eaten for two days.'

He must have sold all his plants that day, because in the evening I saw him at the country liquor shop, tippling away— and all on an empty stomach, I presume!

12 March

Mrs Biggs tells me that someone slipped into her garden yesterday morning while she was out, and removed all her geraniums!

'The most honest of people won't hesitate to steal flowers— or books,' I remark carelessly. 'Never mind, Mrs Biggs, you can have some of my geraniums. I bought them yesterday.'

'That's extremely kind of you, Mr Bond. And you've only just put them down, I can tell,' she says, spotting the cuttings in the Dalda tins.* 'No, I couldn't deprive you—'

'I'll get you some,' I offer, and generously surrender half the geraniums, vowing that if ever I come across that young man again, I'll get him to recover all the plants he sold elsewhere.

19 March

Vinod, now selling newspapers, arrives as I am pouring myself a beer under the cherry tree. It's a warm day and I can see he is thirsty.

'Can I have a drink of water?' he asks.

'Would you like some beer?'

'Yes, sir!'

As I have an extra bottle, I pour him a glass and he squats

---

* Dalda switched over to plastic containers a few years later.

on the grass near the old wall and brings me up to date on the local gossip. There are about fifty papers in his shoulder-bag, yet to be delivered.

'You may feel drowsy after some time,' I warn. 'Don't leave your papers in the wrong houses.'

'Nothing to worry about,' he says, emptying the glass and gazing fondly at the bottle sparkling in the spring sunshine.

'Have some more,' I tell him, and go indoors to see what Prem was making for lunch. (Stuffed gourds, fried brinjal slices, pillau-rice. Prem was in a good mood, preparing my favourite dishes. Had I upset him, he would have given me string beans.) Returning to the garden, I find Vinod well into his second glass of beer. Half of Barlowganj and all of Jharipani (the next village), are snarling and cursing, waiting for their newspapers.

'Your customers must be getting impatient,' I remark. 'Surely they want to know the result of the cricket test.'

'Oh, they heard it on the radio. This is the morning edition. I can deliver it in the evening.'

I went indoors and had my lunch with little Raki, and asked Prem to give Vinod something to eat. When I came outside again, he was stretched out under the cherry tree, burping contentedly.

'Thank you for the lunch,' he said, and closed his eyes and went to sleep.

He'd gone by evening but his bag of papers was resting against my front door.

'He's left his papers behind,' I remarked to Prem.

'Oh, he'll deliver them tomorrow, along with tomorrow's paper. He'll say the mail-bus was late, due to a landslide.'

In the evening I walk through the old bazaar and linger in front of a Tibetan shop, gazing at the brassware, coloured stones, amulets, masks; I am about to pass on, when I catch a glimpse of the girl who looks after the shop. Two soft brown eyes in a round jade-smooth face. A hesitant smile.

I step inside. I have never cared much for Tibetan handicrafts, but beautiful jade eyes are different.

'Can I look around? I want to buy a present for a friend.'

I look around. She helps me, by displaying bangles, necklaces, rings—all on the assumption that my friend is a young lady.

I choose the more frightening of two devil masks, and promise to come again for the pair to it.

On the way home I meet Miss Bun.

'When shall I come?' she asks, pirouetting on the road.

'Next year.'

'Next year!' Her pretty mouth falls open.

'That's right,' I say. 'You've just lost the election.'

31 March

Miss Bun hasn't been for several days. This morning I find her washing clothes at the public tap. She gives me a quick smile as I pass.

'It's nice to see you hard at work,' I remark.

She looks quickly to left and right, then says, 'It's punishment, because I bought new bangles with the money you gave me.'

I hurry on down the road.

During the afternoon siesta I am roused by someone knocking on the door. A slim boy, with thick hair and bushy eyebrows is standing there. I don't know him, but his eyes remind me of someone.

He tells me he is Miss Bun's older brother. At a guess, he would be only a year or two older than her.

'Come in,' I say. It's best to be friendly! What could he possibly want?

He produces a bag of samosas and puts them down on my bedside table.

'My sister cannot come this week. I will bring you samosas instead. Is that all right?'

'Oh, sure. Sit down, sit down. So you're Master Bun. It's nice to know you.'

He sits down on the edge of the bed and studies the picture on the wall—a print of Kurosawa's *Wave*.

'Shall I pay you now for the samosas?' I ask.

'No, no, whenever you like.'

'And do you go to school or college?'

'No, I help my father in the bakery. Are you ill, sir?'

'No. What makes you think so?'

'Because you were lying down.'

'Well, I like lying down. It's better than standing up. And I do get a headache if I read or write for too long.'

He offers to give me a head massage, and I submit to his ministrations for about five minutes. The headache is now much worse, but I pay for both massage and samosas and tell him he can come again—preferably next year.

My next visitor is Constable Ghanshyam Singh, who tells me that the SP has extracted confessions from a couple of thieves simply by making them stand for hours and listen to him reciting his poetry. I know our police have a reputation for torturing suspects, but I think this is carrying things a bit too far.

'And what about your transfer?' I ask.

'As soon as those poems are published in the *Weekly*.'

'I'll do my best,' I promise.

They appeared in the Bhopal *Weekly*.

And a year later, when I was editing *Imprint*, I was able to publish one of the SP's poems. He has always maintained that if I'd published more of them, the magazine would never have folded.

A note on Miss Bun:

Little Miss Bun is fond of bed,
But she keeps a cash-box in her head.

8 April

Rev. Biggs at the door, book in hand.

'I won't take up your time, Mr Bond. But I thought it was time I returned your Butterfly book.'

'My butterfly book?'

'Yes, thank you very much. I enjoyed it a great deal.'

Mr Biggs hands me the book on butterflies, a handsomely illustrated volume. It isn't my book, but if Mr Biggs insists on giving me someone else's book, who am I to quibble? He'd never find the right owner, anyway.

'By the way, have you seen Mrs Biggs?' he asks.

'No, not this morning, sir.'

'She went off without telling me. She's always doing things like that. Very irritating.'

After he has gone, I glance at the fly-leaf of the book. The name-plate says W. Biggs. So it's one of his own . . . .

A little later Mrs Biggs comes by.

'Have you seen Will?' she asks.

'He was here about fifteen minutes ago He was looking for you.'

'Oh, he knew I'd gone to the garden shed. How tiresome! I suppose he's wandered off somewhere.'

'Never mind, Mrs Biggs, he'll make his way home when he gets hungry. A good lunch will always bring a wanderer home. By the way, I've got his book on butterflies. Perhaps you'd return it to him for me? And he shouldn't lend it to just anyone, you know. It's a valuable book, you don't want to lose it.'

'I'm sure it was quite safe with you, Mr Bond.'

Books always are, of course. On principle, I never steal another man's books. I might take his geraniums or his old school tie, but I wouldn't deprive him of his books. Or the song or melody or dream he lives by. And I wrote a little lullaby for Raki:

Little one, don't be afraid of this big river.
Be safe in these warm arms for ever.
Grow tall, my child, be wise and strong.
But do not take from any man his song.
Little one, don't be afraid of this dark night.
Walk boldly as you see the truth and light.
Love well, my child, laugh all day long,
But do not take from any man his song.

16 April

Is there something about the air at this height that makes people light-headed, absent-minded? Ten years from now I will probably be as forgetful as Mr Biggs. I must climb the next

51

mountain before I forget where it is.

*

Outline for a story:
Someone lives in a small hut near a spring, within sound of running water. He never leaves the place, except to walk into the town for books, post, and supplies. 'Don't you ever get bored here?' I asked. 'Do you never wish to leave?' 'No,' he replies, and tells me of his experience in the desert, when for two days and two nights (the limit of human endurance in regard to thirst), he went without water. On the second night, half dead, lying in the open beneath the stars, he dreamt of just such a spring in the mountains, and it was as though it gave him spiritual sustenance. So later, when he was fully recovered, he went in search of the spring (which he was sure existed), and found it while hiking in the Himalayas. He knew that as long as he remained by the spring he would never feel unsafe; it was where his guardian-spirit lived . . . .

And so I feel safe near my own spring, my own mountain, for this is where my guardian-spirit lives too.

16 April

Visited the Tibetan shop and bought a small brass vase encrusted with pretty stones.

I'd no intention of buying anything, but the girl smiled at me as I passed, and then I just had to go in; and once in, I couldn't just stand there, a fatuous grin on my face.

I had to buy something. And a vase is always a good thing to buy. If you don't like it, you can give it away.

If she smiles at me every time I pass, I shall probably build up a collection of vases.

She isn't a girl, really; she's probably about thirty. I suppose she has a husband who smuggles Chinese goods in from Nepal, while her children—'charity cases'—go to one of the posh public schools; but she's fresh and pretty, and then of course I don't have many young women smiling at me these days. I shall be forty-three next month.

17 April

Miss Bun still smiles at me, even though I frown at her when we pass.

This afternoon she brought me samosas and a rose.

'Where's your brother?' I asked gruffly. 'He has more to talk about.'

'He's busy in the bakery. See, I've brought you a rose.'

'How much did it cost?'

'Don't be silly. It's a present.'

'Thanks. I didn't know you grew roses.'

'I don't. It's from the school garden.'

'Well, thank you anyway. You actually stole something on my behalf!'

'Where shall I put it?'

I found my new vase, filled it with fresh water, placed the rose in it, and set it down on my dressing-table.

'It leaks,' remarked Miss Bun.

'My vase?' I was incredulous.

'See, the water's spreading all over your nice table.'

She was right, of course. Water from the bottom of the vase was running across the varnished wood of great-grandmother's old rosewood dressing-table. The stain, I felt sure, would be permanent.

'But it's a new vase!' I protested.

'Someone must have cheated you. Why did you buy it without looking properly?'

'Well, you see, I didn't buy it actually. Someone gave it to me as a present.'

I fumed inwardly, vowing never again to visit the brassware shop. Never trust a smiling woman! I prefer Miss Bun's scowl.

'Do you want the vase?' she asks.

'No. Take it away.'

She places the rose on my pillow, throws the water out of the window, and drops the vase into her cloth shopping-bag.

'What will you do with it?' I ask.

'I'll seal the leak with flour,' she says.

21 April

A clear fresh morning after a week of intermittent rain. And what a morning for birds! Three doves acourting, a cuckoo calling, a bunch of mynas squabbling, and a pair of king-crows doing Swedish exercises.

I find myself doing exercises of an original nature, devised by Master Bun; these consist of various contortions of the limbs which, he says, are good for my sex drive.

'But I don't want a sex drive,' I tell him. 'I want something that will take my mind *off* sex.'

So he gives me another set of exercises, which consist mostly of deep breathing.

'Try holding your breath for five minutes,' he suggests.

'I know of someone who committed suicide by doing just that.'

'Then hold it for two minutes.'

I take a deep breath and last only a minute.

'No good,' he says. 'You have to relax more.'

'Well, I am tired of trying to relax. It doesn't work this way. What I need is a good meal.'

And Prem obliges by serving up my favourite kofta curry and rice. Satiated, I have no problem in relaxing for the rest of the afternoon.

28 April

Master Bun wears a troubled expression.

'It's about my sister,' he says.

'What about her?' I ask, fearing the worst.

'She has run away.'

'That's bad. On her own?'

'No . . . . With a professor.'

'That should be all right. Professors are usually respectable people. Maths or English?'

'I don't know. He has a wife and children.'

'Then obviously he hasn't taken them along.'

'He has taken her to Roorkee. My sister is an innocent girl.'

'Well, there *is* a certain innocence about her,' I say, recalling Nabokov's *Lolita*. 'Maybe the professor wants to adopt her.'

'But she's a virgin.'

'Then she must be rescued! Why are you here, talking to me about it, when you should be rushing down to Roorkee?'

'That's why I've come. Can you lend me the bus fare?'

'Better still, I'll come with you. We must rescue the professor—sorry, I mean your sister!'

1 May

> *To Roorkee, to Roorkee, to find a sweet girl,*
> *Home again, home again, oh what a whirl!*

We did everything except find Miss Bun. Our first evening in Roorkee we roamed the bazaar and the canal banks; the second day we did the rounds of the University, the regimental barracks, and the headquarters of the Boys' Brigade. We made enquiries from all the bakers in Roorkee (many of them known to Master Bun), but none of them had seen his sister. On the college campus we asked for the professor, but no one had heard of him either.

Finally we bought platform tickets and sat down on a bench at the end of the railway platform and watched the arrivals and departures of trains, and the people who got on and off; we saw no one who looked in the least like Miss Bun. Master Bun bought an astrological guide from the station bookstall, and studied his sister's horoscope to see if that might help, but it didn't. At the same bookstall, hidden under a pile of pirated Harold Robbins novels, I found a book of mine that had been published ten years earlier. No one had bought it in all that time. I replaced it at the top of the pile. Never lose hope!

On the third day we returned to Barlowganj and found Miss Bun at home.

She had gone no further than Dehra's Paltan Bazaar, it seemed, and had ditched the professor there, having first made him buy her three dress pieces, two pairs of sandals, a sandalwood hair brush, a bottle of scent, and a satchel for her schoolbooks.

5 May

And now it's Mr Biggs's turn to disappear.

'Have you seen our Will? asks Mrs Biggs at my gate.

'Not this morning, Mrs Biggs.'

'I can't find him anywhere. At breakfast he said he was going out for a walk, but nobody knows where he went, and he isn't in the school compound, I've just enquired. He's been gone over three hours!'

'Don't worry, Mrs Biggs. He'll turn up. Someone on the hillside must have asked him in for a cup of tea, and he's sitting there talking about the crocodile he shot in Orissa.'

But at lunchtime Mr Biggs hadn't returned; and that was alarming, because Mr Biggs had never been known to miss his favourite egg curry and pillau rice.

We organized a search. Prem and I walked the length of the Barlowganj bazaar, and even lodged an unofficial report with Constable Ghanshyam. No one had seen him in the bazaar. Several members of the school staff combed the hillside without picking up the scent.

Mid-afternoon, while giving my negative report to Mrs Biggs, I heard a loud thumping coming from the direction of her storeroom.

'What's all that noise downstairs?' I asked.

'Probably rats. I don't hear anything.'

I ran downstairs and opened the storeroom door, there was Mr Biggs looking very dusty and very disgruntled; he wanted to know why the devil (the first time he'd taken the devil's name in vain), Mrs Biggs had shut him up for hours. He'd gone into the storeroom in search of an old walking-stick, and Mrs Biggs, seeing the door open, had promptly bolted it, failing to hear her husband's cries for immediate release. But for Mr Bond's presence of mind, he averred, he might have been discovered years later, a mere skeleton!

The cook was still out hunting for him, so Mr Biggs had his egg curry cold. Still in a foul mood, he sat down and wrote a letter to his sister in Tunbridge Wells, asking her to send out a hearing-aid for Mrs Biggs.

Constable Ghanshyam turned up in the evening, to inform

me that Mr Biggs had last been seen at Rajpur, in the foothills, in the company of several gypsies!

'Never mind,' I said. 'These old men get that way. One last fling, one last romantic escapade, one last tilt at the windmill. If you have a dream, Ghanshyam, don't let them take it away from you.'

He looked puzzled, but went on to tell me that he was being transferred to Bareilly jail, where they keep those who have been found guilty but of unsound mind. It's a reward, no doubt, for his services in getting the SP's poems published.

*

These journal entries date back some twenty years. What happened to Miss Bun? Well, she finally opened a beauty parlour in New Delhi, but I still can't tell you where it is, or give you her name.

Two or three years later, Mrs Biggs was laid to rest near her old friends in the Mussoorie cemetery. Rev. Biggs was flown home to Turnbridge Wells; his sister gave him a solid tombstone, so that he wasn't tempted to get up and wander off somewhere, in search of crocodiles.

A lot can happen in twenty years, and unfortunately not all of it gets recorded. 'Little Raki' is today a married man!

A Station for Scandal

SIMLA, EVEN IN the days of Mrs Hauksbee, was never so promiscuous. Simla, after all, was teeming with officials and empire-builders and ambitious young civil servants. If there wasn't room for them in Simla, they went to Nainital, capital of the United Provinces.

But Mussoorie was non-official.

It was not a summer capital. You could live there without feeling that the Viceroy or the Governor was looking over your shoulder. Those who made their way to Mussoorie did so in order to get as far as possible from viceroys and governors. It was where you went to 'do your own thing', indulge a secret love, or build a cottage for your mistress, far from the stern and censorious eyes of your superior officers. And sometimes the superior officers turned up too, hoping to get away from their junior officer. And if ever the twain met, well, they looked the other way . . . .

Mussoorie is smaller than Simla, all length and no breadth, but from Clouds End in the west to Jabarkhet in the east, it is all of twelve miles, straddling the ridge overlooking the two great rivers, the Ganga and the Jamuna, which are silver slipstreams across the plains below. There is room enough for private lives, for discreet affairs conducted over picnic baskets set down beneath the deodars.

Some years ago I received a letter from a reader in England, wanting to know if there were any Maxwells still living in Mussoorie. He was a Maxwell himself, he said, by his father's first marriage. From what he knew of the family history, there ought to have been several Maxwells by the second marriage, and he wanted to get in touch with them.

He was very frank and mentioned that his father had

given up a brilliant career in the Indian Civil Service to marry a fifteen-year-old Muslim girl. He had met the girl in Madras, changed his religion to facilitate the marriage, and then—to avoid 'scandal'—had made his home with her in Mussoorie. His first wife had returned to England with her children.

Although there are no longer any Maxwells in Mussoorie, my neighbour, Miss Bean confirmed that Mr Maxwell's children from his second wife had in fact grown up on the station, each inheriting a considerable property. The old gentleman is buried in the Mussoorie cemetery. The children emigrated, but one granddaughter returned to Mussoorie a few years ago, on a honeymoon with her fourth husband, thus keeping up the family tradition.

Mussoorie, queen of the hills, took this sort of thing in its stride.

The station's reputation was well established as far back as October 1884, when the correspondent of the Calcutta *Statesman* wrote to his paper:

> Last Sunday a sermon was delivered by the Reverend Mr Hackett, belonging to the Church Mission Society; he chose for his text Ezekiel 18th and 2nd verse; the latter clause, 'The fathers have eaten sour grapes and set their children's teeth on edge.' The Reverend gentleman discoursed upon the 'highly immoral tone of society up here, that it far surpassed any other hill station in the scale of morals; that ladies and gentlemen after attending church proceeded to a drinking shop, a restaurant adjoining the Library and there indulged freely in *pegs*, not one but many; that at a fancy Bazaar held this season, a lady stood up on a chair and offered her kisses to gentlemen at Rs 5 each. What would they think of such a state of society at Home? But this was not all. Married ladies and married gents formed friendship and associations which tended to no *good* purpose, and set a bad example.'

The poor Reverend preached to no purpose, and it was perhaps just as well that he was not alive in the year 1933, when a lady stood up at a benefit show and auctioned a single kiss for which a gentleman paid Rs 300. (The *Statesman* correspondent had nothing to say on that occasion; his silence was in itself a comment on the changing times.)

Mussoorie was probably at its gayest in the Thirties. Ballrooms, skating-rinks and cinema-halls flourished. Beauty salons sprang up along the Mall. An old advertisement in my possession announces the superiority of 'Freda' in the art of permanent waving; she was assisted by Miss Harvey, 'late of "Lucille", Bedford'.

The war was to change all this; and by the time independence came to India, most of the European and Anglo-Indian residents had sold their homes and gone away. Only a few stayed on— elderly folk like Miss Bean, who had spent her life here, and others whose meagre incomes did not permit them to go away.

I wonder what brought me back to Mussoorie. True, I had sometimes been here as a child; and my mother's people had lived in Dehradun, in the valley below. When I returned to India, still a young man in my twenties (I had spent only four years in England), I lived in Delhi and Dehra for a few years; and then, without quite knowing why, I found myself visiting the hill-station, calling on the oldest resident, Miss Bean, and being told by her that the upper portion of her cottage was to let. On an impulse, I rented it.

That was ten years ago, and Miss Bean has gone to her maker, but here I am, still living in the cottage and keeping it from falling down.

Perhaps I really wanted to come back to my beginnings. Because it was in Mussoorie in 1933 (the Year of the Kissing) that my parents first met and enjoyed a typical hill-station affair.

I have a photograph of my father and mother, on horseback, riding along the Camel's Back Road not far from the cemetery gate. He was thirty-six then, and had just given up a tea-estate manager's job; she was barely twenty, taking a nurse's training at the Cottage Hospital, just below Gun Hill. A few months later they were husband and wife, living in the heat and dust of Alwar state. I was not born in Mussoorie, but I am pretty sure I had my beginnings there.

There is something in the air of the place—especially in October and November—that is conducive to romance and passion. Miss Bean told me that as a girl she'd had many suitors, and if she did not marry it was more from procrastination than from being passed over. While on all sides elopements and broken marriages were making hill-station life exciting, she managed to remain single. She was probably helped in this by her father's reputation for being a very good shot with pistol and Lee-Enfield rifle. She taught elocution in one of the many schools that flourished (and still flourish) in Mussoorie. There is a protective atmosphere about an English public school; an atmosphere which, although it protects one from the outside world, often exposes one to the hazards within the system.

The schools were not without their own scandals. Mrs Fennimore, the wife of a schoolmaster at Oak Grove, got herself entangled in a defamation suit, each hearing of which grew more and more distasteful to her husband. Unable to stand the whole weary and sordid business, Mr Fennimore hit upon a solution. Loading his revolver, he moved to his wife's bedside and shot her through the head. For no accountable reason he put the weapon under her pillow—obviously no one could have mistaken the death for suicide—and then, going to his study, he leaned over his rifle and shot himself.

Ten years later, in the same school, the headmaster's wife was arrested for attempted murder. She had fired at, and wounded, a junior mistress. The case was later hushed up; the motive remains obscure.

But it was on 25 July 1927, at the height of the season and in the heart of the town, that there took place the double tragedy that set the station agog. It all happened in broad daylight and in a full boarding-house, Zephyr Hall.

Shortly after noon the boarders were startled into brisk activity when a shot rang out from one of the rooms, followed by screams. Other shots followed in quick succession. Those boarders who happened to be in the public rooms or on the verandas dived for the safety of their own apartments and bolted the doors. One unhappy boarder, however, ignorant of where the man with the gun might be, decided to take no chances and came round a corner with his hands held well above his head—only to run straight into the levelled pistol. Even the man who held it, and who had just shot his own wife, couldn't help laughing.

Mr Owen, the gentleman with the gun, killed his wife, wounded his daughter, and finally shot himself. His was the first Christian cremation in Mussoorie, performed in compliance with his wishes expressed long before his dramatic end.

This event had a strange sequel, at least for me.

Last summer, while I was taking a walk along the Mall, I was stopped by a stranger, a small man with pale-blue eyes and thinning hair. He must have been over sixty. Accompanying him was a woman of about thirty, whom he introduced as his wife. He apologized for detaining me, and said, 'But you look as though you have been here for some time. Can you tell me where Miss Garlah lives?'

Miss Garlah, another old resident, is the Secretary of the Cemetery Committee, 'house-proud', so to speak, because a visiting representative of the British High Commission once declared that the Mussoorie cemetery was the best-kept 'old' cemetery in northern India.

I gave directions to the visitor, and then asked him if he was visiting Mussoorie for the first time. He seemed to welcome the enquiry and showed an eagerness to talk.

'It's nearly fifty years since I was last here,' he said. And he gestured towards the ruins of Zephyr Hall, once the most fashionable boarding-house in the hill-station and now occupied by poor squatters and their families. 'That was where we lived for a couple of years. That was where my poor mother died . . . .'

My mind was alive with conjecture and now something seemed to fall into place. 'Not—not Mrs Owen?' I ventured to ask.

'That's right. But surely you're too young to remember.'

'I heard about it,' I lied. Actually, I had a couple of old newspaper clippings on the case.

'My father had a sudden brainstorm. He shot and killed my mother. My sister was badly wounded, but she recovered.'

'And what about you?' I asked. I couldn't remember reading about a son.

'I was at school in England, just fourteen years old. They'd sent me to England only a few months before it happened. I heard about it much later. Naturally, I couldn't attend my mother's funeral, and I've had to wait fifty years before I could come and see her grave. I know she'd have wanted me to come.'

He took my telephone number and promised to look me up before he left Mussoorie. But I did not see him again. After a few days I began to wonder if I had really met the survivor of a fifty-year-old tragedy, or if he had been just another of the hill-station's ghosts. But only a couple of weeks back, when I was walking along the cemetery's lowest terrace looking for a grave that Miss Garlah said needed to be identified (she couldn't manage the steep path down to the bottom terrace), I received confirmation that Mr Owen Junior had indeed visited Mussoorie and that he had found his mother's grave.

There before me was the grave of Mrs Owen, victim of her husband's brainstorm. And a new plaque had been set into the stone, with the inscription: 'Mother Dear, I am Here'.

1976

It Must be the Mountains*
A thirty-minute play for radio

Characters
Miss Mackenzie: an active old lady
Colonel Wilkie: retired from the Indian Army
Anil: an Indian schoolboy
An old Bearer: (or manservant)
(and a narrator for the opening passage)

Sound effects required
Birdsong, including sound of woodpecker
Doors and windows which must sometimes be opened or closed
Footsteps on gravel
A creaking gate
A boy scrambling through shrubbery
Sound of digging
A rattle of teacups

Notes for guidance
The Colonel and Miss Mackenzie would of course speak with English accents. The boy would speak fairly clear English, *without* any marked Indian accent—he studies at an English-medium school; the Bearer would speak English with difficulty and slow deliberation—but he doesn't have to say much.

The term 'Miss' rather than 'Ma'am' is used by schoolboys in

---

* This little play for radio (never broadcast or published) was my only attempt at play-writing. It was written during the period of these journals, and the characters are based on Miss Bean, who shared my cottage for a time, and of course Sir Edmund. Anil was a real boy—I believe he did become a botanist!

India when addressing a lady teacher—irrespective of whether she's a Miss or Mrs.

NARRATOR	:	The year is 1968. Miss Mackenzie, who is eighty-six years old, is the oldest resident of a small hill-station in northern India. She has been living there since 1904. One of a handful of British people still living in the hills of India, she has known more prosperous days. She has been a spinster all her life, and lives alone in a small cottage near a forest of oak and rhododendron. Her old bearer, who is almost eighty himself, is her only companion, apart from the occasional visitor.

(BIRDSONG, DOMINATED BY THE KNOCKING OF A WOODPECKER)

MISS MACKENZIE	:	Bearer! [Pause] Bearer! [Pause] Oh, what a deaf old codger he's become. *Bear-er!*
BEARER	:	Yes, missy-baba.
MISS M	:	Oh, do come here and help me open this window. I can hear a woodpecker outside. I must know where it is. And I've told you a hundred times not to call me *missy-baba*—I stopped wearing pigtails seventy years ago!
BEARER	:	Yes, missy-baba. The window.
MISS M	:	Come on then—push!

(PAUSE. BOTH STRAIN AT THE WINDOW)

MISS M	:	No, it won't open. You *are* a feeble old man. Never mind . . . I'm going out into the garden. Its good to have the sun again after two days of rain and hail.

(DOOR OPENS, BIRDSONG IS LOUDER)

MISS M	:	Oh, it is lovely outside. Just listen to the birds. There's a blackbird—and a whistling-thrush. And there's the woodpecker, up at the top of that old spruce. Can you see it, Bearer?
BEARER	:	No, missy-baba, I cannot see as well as you.
MISS M	:	No, I suppose not. The Mackenzies always had good eyesight.
BEARER	:	Your father's eyesight was very good, missy-baba.
MISS M	:	And so is mine, thank God. Yes—I can see Colonel Wilkie coming down the road, though he hasn't seen *me* as yet. Unless, of course, he's trying to avoid me. Colonel Wilkie! [Pause] *Colonel!*
COLONEL WILKIE	:	[startled] Oh!—ah—why, it's Mary! Good morning, Mary. Lovely day, isn't it?
MISS M	:	Gorgeous. Can you see the woodpecker?
COLONEL	:	No. Where?
MISS M	:	At the top of the spruce.
COLONEL	:	I can't see a thing.
MISS M	:	I thought not. Can you *hear* it?

(PAUSE. WOODPECKER KNOCKS FAINTLY)

COLONEL	:	No. I'm afraid my hearing isn't so good now, Mary. Wait a minute, though—

(LOUD KNOCKING)

		I *do* hear something now, Mary.
MISS M	:	That's Bearer chopping wood. But never mind. Are you coming in, or are you on your way to the bazaar?
COLONEL	:	Well, I wasn't going anywhere in particular. But I couldn't sit at home on a day like this. I'll come in, I think.
MISS M	:	Do.

(GATE OPENS—CREAKILY. FOOTSTEPS ON GRAVEL)

COLONEL	:	I see your primulas are doing well.
MISS M	:	Yes, but the hail has ruined all my candytuft.
COLONEL	:	A pity. [Pause] Hullo—what's this?
MISS M	:	That's a lupin.
COLONEL	:	No, here in this corner. It's a little bird, Mary. I think it's dead. Must have died from exposure.
MISS M	:	Poor thing. Let me see, Colonel. Are you sure it's dead? [Pause] I think it's still breathing.
COLONEL	:	You're right. It's still alive.
MISS M	:	Well, let's take it inside and put it near the stove. Perhaps the warmth will revive it. Such a pretty little redstart!
COLONEL	:	I think it's a flycatcher.
MISS M	:	It's not a flycatcher, it's a redstart.
COLONEL	:	I'm *sure* it's a red-breasted flycatcher.
MISS M	:	Nonsense! But we mustn't stand here arguing. Let's take it inside.

(PAUSE. DOOR OPENS)

MISS M	:	Bearer—Bearer!
BEARER	:	Missy-baba?
MISS M	:	Oh, you did startle me! Bearer, put the kettle on for tea. And another cup for the Colonel-sahib. Do sit down, Colonel.
COLONEL	:	I don't think you have a chair large enough for me, Mary. I must say you go in for rather small-sized furniture.
MISS M	:	My furniture is perfectly normal. It's your own circumference that's abnormal. When you arrived a little while ago, I feared for an eclipse of the sun!
COLONEL	:	Now, Mary, that's most unkind. And I wish

		you'd call me Horace.
MISS M	:	I never cared for the name. I prefer to call you Colonel. There, I've put the redstart near the stove. I do think it's breathing more easily now.
COLONEL	:	A redstart should have some white on its head.
MISS M	:	You're thinking of the white-capped redstart. This is an ordinary redstart.
COLONEL	:	I didn't know a redstart had so much red on its—er—its—er—
MISS M	:	Bottom.
COLONEL	:	Exactly. You put these things so well, Mary. Anyway, I think it s a flycatcher.
MISS M	:	You *are* stubborn—always have been.
COLONEL	:	Oh, I don't know about that. You're rather stubborn yourself. It must be the Scot in you.
MISS M	:	And it must be the Colonel in you.
COLONEL	:	You should have gone home to England like everyone else, twenty years ago. What made you stay on in India?
MISS M	:	Because I wanted to. What makes anyone do anything? Because they want to—unless they're complete morons.
COLONEL	:	Yes, but don't you ever feel lonely?
MISS M	:	Don't you?
COLONEL	:	I suppose I do, at times.
MISS M	:	And what do you do about it?
COLONEL	:	Oh, I don't know. If I'm feeling homesick, I can listen to the BBC. But even that isn't what it used to be—nothing like the good old days of Tommy Handley and Colonel Chinstrap.
MISS M	:	Those weren't good old days, Colonel. That was the War.
COLONEL	:	Yes, I know it was, my dear, and the War years were the best years of my life.

Miss M	:	Did you kill anyone?
Colonel	:	I haven't the faintest idea. I was in the artillery. But it was never as bloody as the first War. Even wars aren't what they used to be—
Miss M	:	Do you think there'll be another?
Colonel	:	Can't say. I'd be too old for it, anyway, But I must say the years haven't taken much out of you, Mary. You're still very spry.
Miss M	:	It's living in the mountains.
Colonel	:	Yes, it must be the mountains. I wish I'd spent more or my life at this height, then perhaps I wouldn't have been racked with rheumatism. But haven't you ever wanted a change?
Miss M	:	Oh, I've been away from time to time. I lived in the plains for a couple of years, when I was younger; and I thought, once, of going to England. But I don't have anyone in England now—and there's something about the mountains—something that gets into your blood—that draws you back to them, time and again. Once you have lived with mountains . . . .
Colonel	:	Kipling said something like that. He was describing the smell of the Himalayas, and he said—'once it creeps into the blood of a man, that man will at the last, forgetting all else, return to the hills to die' . . . [Pause] That flycatcher looks as though it's recovering.
Miss M	:	Yes, it's stretching its wings. What a pretty little bird a redstart is!
Colonel	:	No doubt, but this one's a flycatcher.
Miss M	:	Nonsense!

(SOMEONE COMES CRASHING THROUGH THE SHRUBBERY OUTSIDE)

MISS M	:	Oh, there's someone in the garden!
COLONEL	:	Sounds like an entire regiment.
MISS M	:	Worse still—it's a schoolboy!
COLONEL	:	I'll send him off!
MISS M	:	No, let *me* deal with him. You remain here, Colonel. [Pause] Who's there? What are you up to, boy?
ANIL	:	Oh! Er—good morning, miss.
MISS M	:	[Severely] Good morning. Would you mind moving out of my flower-bed?
ANIL	:	Oh, I'm sorry, miss.
MISS M	:	You're trespassing.
ANIL	:	Er—yes, miss.
MISS M	:	And you ought to be in school at this time.
ANIL	:	Yes, miss.
MISS M	:	Then what are you doing here?
ANIL	:	Picking flowers, miss.
MISS M	:	Picking my flowers!
ANIL	:	Oh no, not yours! I was picking wild flowers.
MISS M	:	Oh, I see. Well, that's different [softening]. Do you like flowers?
ANIL	:	Yes. I'm going to be a botan—a botanitist!
MISS M	:	You mean a botanist.
ANIL	:	Yes, miss.
MISS M	:	Well, that's unusual. Most boys at your age want to be airmen or soldiers or singing-stars. But you want to be a botanist. Well, well. There's still some hope left for the world. And do you know the names of the flowers you've been gathering?
ANIL	:	This is a *Bukhilo*, that's an Indian name. It means a prayer, and it's offered to God when you pray to Him. Of course you can offer it without praying, a flower is as good a prayer. But I don't know what *this* is . . . .
MISS M	:	It's a wild primrose. And that other plant is a larkspur, but it isn't wild, it's a plant from my garden.

ANIL	:	I'm very sorry. I must have taken it by mistake.
MISS M	:	That's all right. What's your name?
ANIL	:	Anil.
MISS M	:	And where do you live?
ANIL	:	In Delhi, when school closes. My father has a business there.
MISS M	:	Oh, and what's his business?
ANIL	:	Bulbs.
MISS M	:	Flower bulbs?
ANIL	:	Electric bulbs.
MISS M	:	Electric bulbs! You might send me a few, after you go home. Mine are always fusing, and they're so expensive, like everything else these days. Do you have any books on flowers?
ANIL	:	No, miss.
MISS M	:	Well, come in and I'll show you one.
ANIL	:	Thank you, miss.

(PAUSE. A SOUND OF SNORING)

ANIL	:	There's a strange noise inside.
MISS M	:	It's only Colonel Wilkie. He's fallen asleep. Wake up, Colonel.
COLONEL	:	Eh! Oh—ah—I do apologize. Awfully rude of me, Mary. Hullo—who's this?
MISS M	:	This is Anil. He goes to school up on the hill, and he says he wants to be a botanist. Now let me find that book for you, Anil. [Pause] Here we are—*Flora Himaliensis*, published in 1892, and probably the only copy still in India. This is a very valuable book, Anil. No other naturalist has recorded so many wild Himalayan plants. And remember, there are still many flowers and plants which are unknown to the fancy botanists who spend all their time at

		microscopes instead of in the mountains. But perhaps *you'll* do something about that, one day.
ANIL	:	Yes, miss.
COLONEL	:	Do you have any books on *birds*, Mary?
MISS M	:	I don't think so. Why?
COLONEL	:	Well, I thought it might help us settle the question as to whether ours is a redstart or flycatcher.
MISS M	:	There you go again—
ANIL	:	Oh, look, there's a dead bird on the stove!
COLONEL	:	It isn't dead.
MISS M	:	Oh, but it *is* dead, poor thing. It must have died while I was outside, and while *you* were snoring in that chair, Colonel.
COLONEL	:	Well, how was I to know—and what could I have done about it, anyway. I'm not a bird doctor!
MISS M	:	Well, you claim to know a lot about them. [Pause] It's a redstart, Anil. We found it lying in the garden, and tried to revive it, but I suppose we were too late . . . .
COLONEL	:	Poor little flycatcher. Shall I throw it out, Mary?
MISS M	:	Throw it out? Don't be so callous.
COLONEL	:	Well, then, what do you want to do with the bird—stuff it?
MISS M	:	Don't be childish. We'll *bury* it. You'll help me to bury the little bird, won't you, Anil?
ANIL	:	Yes, miss.
MISS M	:	Good. Come with me into the garden, we'll bury it behind the hollyhocks. Are you coming, Colonel?
COLONEL	:	Oh, by all means. Anything to oblige.

(PAUSE. FOOTSTEPS ON GRAVEL)

MISS M	:	Bearer! Oh, here he is. Bearer, have you got

		a spade? He's forgotten what a spade is. There's one over by the kitchen door. Will you fetch it, Anil?
ANIL	:	Yes, miss. [Pause. Footsteps running on gravel] Here you are, miss. Shall I dig a hole?
Miss M	:	Do please. But be careful of the plants.

(SOUND OF DIGGING)

Miss M	:	I think that should be enough. [Pause] Now place the bird in gently. Poor little redstart.
COLONEL	:	[Under his breath] Flycatcher.
Miss M	:	Now cover it with earth and place a couple of big stones on top, so that the jackals can't dig it up. Good.
COLONEL	:	Do you want me to read a service?
Miss M	:	Don't be so facetious!
COLONEL	:	Well, if it's all over, I'd better be going or I won't get any lunch. I'm afraid boarding-houses aren't what they used to be . . . . I wish I could be as independent as you are, Mary. I don't know how you manage it, on your small pension.
Miss M	:	Well, as long as I'm alive and kicking—I'll kick!
COLONEL	:	Oh, I'm sure you will.
Miss M	:	But you've got nothing to grumble about, Colonel. You do quite well at the Lodge.
COLONEL	:	So you think. You should try getting your teeth into the meat they serve up.
Miss M	:	At least you get meat. I can't afford it more than once a week.
COLONEL	:	Yes, Well—I must be off. And thank you for the tea.
Miss M	:	The tea? Good heavens! But you haven't had any tea!
COLONEL	:	Oh, well, don't bother now. I suppose your

		Bearer forgot all about it, or fell asleep over the kettle.
Miss M	:	Oh, I *am* sorry, Colonel.
Colonel	:	Quite all right, my dear, quite all right, Well, goodbye—and I'm sorry about the—er—redstart . . . .
Miss M	:	Goodbye, Colonel. Perhaps it *was* a flycatcher . . . .

(PAUSE. FOOTSTEPS ON GRAVEL, RECEDING)

Miss M	:	Poor old Colonel Wilkie. I'm afraid he's getting on. He needs a little humouring, now and then. [Pause] It does seem a pity to stay indoors on a day like this, but the sun makes me giddy if I stand out in the garden for too long. If I was just a *little* younger, Anil, I could join you in your rambles. And then you wouldn't have any trouble over the names of flowers. Do you know what I'd like to do, if I could be your age again?
Anil	:	What Miss?
Miss M	:	Climb that mountain—that one, standing high above the others, still covered with snow.
Anil	:	How high is it?
Miss M	:	It must be over 12,000 feet. About thirty miles from here, as the crow flies—and I wouldn't mind being a crow, just to get there. Would you?
Anil	:	Not a crow, miss, an eagle.
Miss M	:	I'd settle for a crow—or perhaps a redstart . . . .
Anil	:	Was it really a redstart, or a flycatcher?
Miss M	:	I'm not sure, but I like to tease the Colonel. He hates being contradicted. But we were talking about getting to the mountain. I've always wanted to go there, but there's no

proper road. On the slopes there'll be flowers that you don't get here—the blue gentian and the purple columbine, the anemone and the edelweiss. Gentians are even bluer than the sky on a summer's day.

ANIL : I'll go up there one day.
MISS M : I'm sure you will, if you really want to.
ANIL : I want to go everywhere.
MISS M : Perhaps you will. A boy who stands like that with his hands on his hips usually goes where he wants to.
ANIL : May I come to see you again?
MISS M : Yes, of course.
ANIL : Thank you. I had better go now.
MISS M : Aren't you taking the book?

(PAUSE)

ANIL : Oh. I didn't know that you were—giving it to me, miss.
MISS M : Yes, here you are, it's a present for you.
ANIL : But—I'll be coming to see you again, and I can look at it then. It's so valuable!
MISS M : I know it's valuable, and that's why I'm giving it to you. Otherwise it might only fall into the hands of one of the junk-dealers one day . . . . And don't tell your headmaster about it. He wants the book himself. Only I don't believe he'll read it. And books are meant to be read and used, aren't they?
ANIL : Yes, but—
MISS M : Don't argue. Besides, I may not be here when you come again.
ANIL : Are you going away?
MISS M : I'm not sure.
ANIL : Are you going back to England?
MISS M : No, I couldn't that. I'm too old to start life all over again. England has changed—and

75

		besides, I've no one there—no brothers or sisters. My home is here, Anil—in these hills, among these trees.
ANIL	:	Don't you feel lonely?
MISS M	:	Yes, I do, sometimes—but at my age it would be lonely anywhere. [Pause] There are lots of trees around this cottage, Anil, and trees take away some of the loneliness.
MISS M	:	Goodbye! And mind the nasturtiums!
ANIL	:	Goodbye!

(FOOTSTEPS AND THE GATE CREAKS. PAUSE)

| MISS M | : | I suppose I'd better go in and see what's happened to Bearer. Oh, I feel quite exhausted. It's been a busy morning—two visitors, and the death of a redstart. |

(PAUSE)

| MISS M | : | Bearer! |

(RATTLE OF TEACUPS)

BEARER	:	The tea, missy-baba.
MISS M	:	The tea! Oh, Bearer, you are a funny old thing. They've all *gone*, Bearer. The Colonel-sahib has gone, and so has the boy. And I'm not going to sit down and drink it all by myself. Do take it away.
BEARER	:	Yes, missy-baba.

(DOOR CLOSES)

| MISS M | : | If the Colonel hadn't gone, or if the boy had still been here, I might have had some tea. [Pause] Oh, I do wish there was someone to talk to . . . . But I mustn't be thinking on |

those lines, or the loneliness will start closing
in again . . . . I know—I'll do some gardening.
What was it the boy said? A flower is as
good as a prayer . . . . Well, then—never
mind the sun—I'll be gardening.

MOUNTAINS
IN MY
BLOOD

*There
is no
Escape*

How Far is the River?

Between the boy and the river was a mountain. I was a small boy, and it was a small river, but the mountain was big.

The thickly forested mountain hid the river, but I knew it was there and what it looked like; I had never seen the river with my own eyes, but from the villagers I had heard of it, of the fish in its waters, of its rocks and currents and waterfalls, and it only remained for me to touch the water and know it personally.

I stood in front of our house on the hill opposite the mountain, and gazed across the valley, dreaming of the river. I was barefooted; not because I couldn't afford shoes, but because I felt free with my feet bare, because I liked the feel of warm stones and cool grass, because not wearing shoes saved me the trouble of taking them off.

It was eleven o'clock and I knew my parents wouldn't be home till evening. There was a loaf of bread I could take with me, and on the way I might find some fruit. Here was the chance I had been waiting for: it would not come again for a long time, because it was seldom that my father and mother visited friends for the entire day. If I came back before dark, they wouldn't know where I had been.

I went into the house and wrapped the loaf of bread in a newspaper. Then I closed all the doors and windows.

The path to the river dropped steeply into the valley, then rose and went round the big mountain. It was frequently used by the villagers, woodcutters, milkmen, shepherds, mule-drivers—but there were no villages beyond the mountain or near the river.

I passed a woodcutter and asked him how far it was to the river. He was a short, powerful man, with a creased and weathered face, and muscles that stood out in hard lumps.

'Seven miles,' he said. 'Why do you want to know?'

'I am going there,' I said.

'Alone?'

'Of course.'

'It will take you three hours to reach it, and then you have to come back. It will be getting dark, and it is not an easy road.'

'But I'm a good walker,' I said, though I had never walked further than the two miles between our house and my school. I left the woodcutter on the path, and continued down the hill.

It was a dizzy, winding path, and I slipped once or twice and slid into a bush or down a slope of slippery pine-needles. The hill was covered with lush green ferns, the trees were entangled in creepers, and a great wild dahlia would suddenly rear its golden head from the leaves and ferns.

Soon I was in the valley, and the path straightened out and then began to rise. I met a girl who was coming from the opposite direction. She held a long curved knife with which she had been cutting grass, and there were rings in her nose and ears and her arms were covered with heavy bangles. The bangles made music when she moved her wrists. It was as though her hands spoke a language of their own.

'How far is it to the river?' I asked.

The girl had probably never been to the river, or she may have been thinking of another one, because she said, 'Twenty miles,' without any hesitation.

I laughed and ran down the path. A parrot screeched suddenly, flew low over my head, a flash of blue and green. It took the course of the path, and I followed its dipping flight, running until the path rose and the bird disappeared amongst the trees.

A trickle of water came down the hillside, and I stopped to drink. The water was cold and sharp but very refreshing. But I was soon thirsty again. The sun was striking the side of the hill, and the dusty path became hotter, the stones scorching my feet. I was sure I had covered half the distance: I had been walking for over an hour.

Presently I saw another boy ahead of me, driving a few goats down the path.

'How far is the river?' I asked.

The village boy smiled and said, 'Oh, not far, just round the next hill and straight down.'

Feeling hungry, I unwrapped my loaf of bread and broke it in two, offering one half to the boy. We sat on the hillside and ate in silence.

When we had finished, we walked on together and began talking; and talking, I did not notice the smarting of my feet, and the heat of the sun, the distance I had covered and the distance I had yet to cover. But after some time my companion had to take another path, and once more I was on my own.

I missed the village boy; I looked up and down the mountain path but no one else was in sight. My own home was hidden from view by the side of the mountain, and there was no sign of the river. I began to feel discouraged. If someone had been with me, I would not have faltered; but alone, I was conscious of my fatigue and isolation.

But I had come more than half way, and I couldn't turn back; I had to see the river. If I failed, I would always be a little ashamed of the experience. So I walked on, along the hot, dusty, stony path, past stone huts and terraced fields, until there were no more fields or huts, only forest and sun and loneliness. There were no men, and no sign of man's influence— only trees and rocks and grass and small flowers—and silence . . . .

The silence was impressive and a little frightening. There was no movement, except for the bending of grass beneath my feet, and the circling of a hawk against the blind blue of the sky.

Then, as I rounded a sharp bend, I heard the sound of water.

I gasped with surprise and happiness, and began to run. I slipped and stumbled, but I kept on running, until I was able to plunge into the snow-cold mountain water.

And the water was blue and white and wonderful.

Four Boys on a Glacier

O<small>N A DAY</small> that promised rain we bundled ourselves into the bus that was to take us to Kapkote (where people lost their caps and coats, punned Anil), the starting-point of our Himalayan trek. I was seventeen at the time, and Anil and Somi were sixteen. Each of us carried a haversack, and we had also brought along a good-sized bedding-roll which, apart from blankets, contained bags of rice and flour, thoughtfully provided by Anil's mother. We had no idea how we would carry the bedding-roll once we started walking, but we didn't worry too much about details.

We were soon in the hills of Kumaon, on a winding road that took us up and up, until we saw the valley and our small town spread out beneath us, the river a silver ribbon across the plain. We took a sharp bend, the valley disappeared, and the mountains towered above us.

At Kapkote we had refreshments and the shopkeeper told us we could spend the night in one of his rooms. The surroundings were pleasant, the hills wooded with deodars, the lower slopes planted with fresh green paddy. At night there was a wind moaning in the trees and it found its way through the cracks in the windows and eventually through our blankets.

Next morning we washed our faces at a small stream near the shop and filled our water bottles for the day's march. A boy from the nearby village approached us, and asked where we were going.

'To the glacier,' said Somi.

'I'll come with you,' said the boy. 'I know the way.'

'You're too small,' said Anil. 'We need someone who can carry our bedding-roll.'

'I'm small but I'm strong,' said the boy, who certainly looked sturdy. He had pink cheeks and a well-knit body.

'See!' he said, and, picking up a rock the size of a football, he heaved it across the stream.

'I think he can come with us,' I said.

And then, we were walking—at first above the little Sarayu river, then climbing higher along the rough mule track, always within sound of the water, which we glimpsed now and then, swift, green and bubbling.

We were at the forest rest-house by six in the evening, after covering fifteen miles. Anil found the watchman asleep in a patch of fading sunlight and roused him. The watchman, who hadn't been bothered by visitors for weeks, grumbled at our intrusion but opened a room for us. He also produced some potatoes from his store, and these were roasted for dinner.

Just as we were about to get into our beds we heard a thud on the corrugated tin roof, and then the sound of someone—or something—scrambling about on the roof. Anil, Somi and I were alarmed; but Bisnu, who was already under the blankets, merely yawned, and turned over on his side.

'It's only a bear,' he said. 'Didn't you see the pumpkins on the roof? Bears love pumpkins.'

For half an hour we had to listen to the bear as it clambered about on the roof, feasting on the watchman's ripe pumpkins. At last there was silence. Anil and I crawled out of our blankets and went to the window. And through the frosted glass we saw a black Himalayan bear ambling across the slope in front of the house.

Our next rest-house lay in a narrow valley, on the banks of the rushing Pindar river, which twisted its way through the mountains. We walked on, past terraced fields and small stone houses, until there were no more fields or houses, only forest and sun and silence.

It was different from the silence of a room or an empty street.

And then, the silence broke into sound—the sound of the river.

Far down in the valley, the Pindar tumbled over itself in its impatience to reach the plains. We began to run; slipped and stumbled, but continued running.

The rest-house stood on a ledge just above the river, and the sound of the water rushing down the mountain-defile could be heard at all times. The sound of the birds, which we had grown used to, was drowned by the sound of the water, but the birds themselves could be seen, many-coloured, standing out splendidly against the dark green forest foliage—the red crowned jay, the paradise flycatcher, the purple whistling thrush and others we could not recognize.

Higher up the mountain, above some terraced land where oats and barley were grown, stood a small cluster of huts. This, we were told by the watchman, was the last village on the way to the glacier. It was, in fact, one of the last villages in India, because if we crossed the difficult passes beyond the glacier, we would find ourselves in Tibet.

Anil asked the watchman about the Abominable Snowman. The Nepalese believe in the existence of the Snowman, and our watchman was Nepalese.

'Yes, I have seen thè yeti,' he told us. 'A great shaggy, flat-footed creature. In the winter, when it snows heavily, he passes the bungalow at night. I have seen his tracks the next morning.'

'Does he come this way in the summer?' asked Somi, anxiously.

'No,' said the watchman. 'But sometimes I have seen the *lidini*. You have to be careful of her.'

'And who is the *lidini*?' asked Anil.

'She is the snow-woman, and far more dangerous. She has the same height as the yeti—about seven feet when her back is straight—and her hair is much longer. Also she has very long teeth. Her feet face inwards, but she can run very fast, especially downhill. If you see a *lidini*, and she chases you, always run in an uphill direction. She tires quickly because of her crooked feet. But when running downhill she has no trouble at all, and you want to be very fast to escape her!'

'Well, we are quite fast,' said Anil with a nervous laugh. 'But it's just a fairy-story, I don't believe a word of it.'

The watchman was most offended, and refused to tell us anything more about snowmen and snow-women. But he helped

Bisnu make a fire, and presented us with a black, sticky sweet, which we ate with relish.

It was a fine, sunny morning when we set out to cover the last seven miles to the glacier. We had expected a stiff climb, but the rest-house was 11,000 feet above sea-level, and the rest of the climb was fairly gradual.

Suddenly, abruptly, there were no more trees. As the bungalow dropped out of sight, the trees and bushes gave way to short grass and little pink and blue alpine flowers. The snow peaks were close now, ringing us in on every side. We passed white waterfalls, cascading hundreds of feet down precipitous rock faces, thundering into the little river. A great white eagle hovered over us.

The hill fell away, and there, confronting us, was a great white field of snow and ice, cradled between two shining peaks. We were speechless for several minutes. Then we proceeded cautiously on to the snow, supporting each other on the slippery surface. We could not go far, because we were quite unequipped for any high-altitude climbing. But it was a satisfying feeling to know that we were the only young men from our town who had walked so far and so high.

The sun was reflected sharply from the snow and we felt surprisingly warm. It was delicious to feel the sun crawling over our bodies, sinking deep into our bones. Meanwhile, almost imperceptibly, clouds had covered some of the peaks, and white mist drifted down the mountain slopes. It was time to return: we would barely make it to the bungalow before it grew dark.

We took our time returning to Kapkote; stopped by the Sarayu river; bathed with the village boys we had seen on the way up; collected strawberries and ferns and wild flowers; and finally said goodbye to Bisnu.

Anil wanted to take Bisnu along with us, but the boy's parents refused to let him go, saying that he was too young for the life of a city.

'Never mind,' said Somi. 'We'll go on another trek next year, and we'll take you with us, Bisnu.'

This promise pleased Bisnu, and he saw us off at the

bus-stop, shouldering our bedding-roll to the end. Then he climbed a pine tree to have a better view of us leaving. We saw him waving to us from the tree as the bus went round the bend from Kapkote, and then the hills were left behind and the plains stretched out below.

Growing up with Trees

DEHRA WAS A good place for trees, and Grandfather's house was surrounded by several kinds—peepul, neem, mango, jack-fruit and papaya. There was also an ancient banyan tree. I grew up amongst these Indian trees, while some of them were planted by Grandfather and grew up with me.

There were two kinds of tree that were of special interest to me—trees that were good for climbing, and trees that provided fruit.

The jack-fruit tree was both these things. The fruit itself—the largest in the world—grew only on the trunk and main branches. It was not my favourite food, and I preferred it cooked as a vegetable. But the tree was large and leafy and easy to climb.

The peepul was a good tree to sit beneath on hot days. Its heart-shaped leaf, sensitive to the slightest breeze, would be flapping gently when the clouds were standing still and not another tree witnessed the least movement in the air. There is a peepul tree in every Indian village, and it is common to see a farmer, tired at the end of an afternoon's toil in the fields, being lulled to sleep by the rustling of its leaves.

A banyan grew behind our house. Its spreading branches, which hung to the ground and took root again, formed a number of twisting passageways which gave me endless pleasure. The tree was older than the house, old_ than my grandparents, as old as the town. I could hide myself in its branches, behind thick green leaves, and spy on the world below. I could read in it, too, propped up against the bole of the tree with *Treasure Island, Huck Finn, The Jungle Books*, David Copperfield,* and English comics like *Wizard* and *Hotspur,* which

---

* I found Kipling's *Second Jungle Book* even more appealing than the first.

were for reading, not just looking at.

The banyan tree was a world in itself, populated with small beasts and large insects. While the leaves were still pink and tender, they would be visited by the delicate map butterfly, who committed her eggs to their care. The 'honey' on the leaves—an edible smear—also attracted the little striped squirrels, who soon grew used to my presence in the tree and became quite bold, accepting peanuts from my hand. Red-headed parrakeets swarmed about the tree early in the mornings.

But the banyan really came to life during the monsoon, when the branches were thick with scarlet figs. These berries were not fit for human consumption, but the many birds that gathered in the tree—gossipy rosy pastors, quarrelsome mynas, cheerful bulbuls and coppersmiths, and sometimes a raucous, bullying crow—feasted on them. And when night fell, and the birds were resting, the dark flying Foxes flapped heavily about the tree, chewing and munching as they clambered over the branches.

One of my favourite trees was the jamun, also known as the Java plum. Its purple astringent fruit ripened during the rains, and then I would join the gardener's young son in its branches, and we would feast like birds on the smooth succulent fruit until our lips and cheeks were stained a bright purple.

The neem (or margosa) was another tree that came into its own during the monsoon rains. The first heavy shower made it shed its small yellow berries, and as they were crushed by passing feet they gave off a strong sweet smell. Its leaves were a pale green, and their fresh, shiny texture added charm to a tree that had many uses. (The gum and oil are used medicinally; the leaves can be cooked as a vegetable; the oil-cake makes an excellent fertilizer; and the green twigs are used as toothbrushes in almost every Indian village.)

Among nocturnal visitors to the jack-fruit and banyan trees was the brainfever bird, whose real name is the hawk-cuckoo. 'Brainfever, brainfever!' it seems to call, and this shrill, nagging cry will keep the soundest of sleepers awake on a hot summer's night.

The British called it the brainfever bird, but there are other names for it. The Marathas called it *paos-ala* which means 'rain is coming'! Perhaps Grandfather's interpretation of its call was the most suitable. According to him, when the bird was tuning up for its main concert, it seemed to say: 'Oh dear, oh dear! How very hot it's getting! We feel it . . . we feel it . . . we feel it!'

Yes, the banyan tree was a noisy place during the rains. If the brainfever bird made music by night, the crickets and cicadas orchestrated during the day. As musicians, the cicadas were in a class by themselves. All through the hot weather their chorus rang through the garden, while a shower of rain, far from damping their spirits, only roused them to a greater choral effort.

The tree-crickets were a band of willing artists who commenced their performance at almost any time of the day but preferably in the evenings. Delicate pale green creatures with transparent green wings, they were hard to find amongst the lush monsoon foliage; but once located, a tap on the bush or leaf on which they sat would put an immediate end to the performance.

At the height of the monsoon, the banyan tree was like an orchestra-pit with the musicians constantly tuning up. Birds, insects and squirrels expressed their joy at the termination of the hot weather and the cool quenching relief of the monsoon.

A toy flute in my hands, I would try adding my shrill piping to theirs. But they thought poorly of my musical ability, for, whenever I piped, the birds and the insects maintained a pained and puzzled silence.

Mountains in my Blood

It was while I was living in England, in the jostle and drizzle of London, that I remembered the Himalayas at their most vivid.   had grown up amongst those great blue and brown mountains; they had nourished my blood; and though I was separated from them by thousands of miles of ocean, plain and desert, I could not rid them from my system. It is always the same with mountains. Once you have lived with them for any length of time, you belong to them. There is no escape.

And so, in London in March, the fog became a mountain mist, and boom of traffic became the boom of the Ganges emerging from the foothills.

I remembered a little mountain path which led my restless feet into a cool, sweet forest of oak and rhododendron, and then on to the windswept crest of a naked hilltop. The hill was called Clouds End. It commanded a view of the plains on one side, and of the snow peaks on the other. Little silver rivers twisted across the valley below, where the rice-fields formed a patchwork of emerald green. And on the hill itself, the wind made a *hoo-hoo-hoo* in the branches of the tall deodars where it found itself trapped.

During the rains, clouds enveloped the valley but left the hill alone, an island in the sky. Wild sorrel grew amongst the rocks, and there were many flowers—convolvulus, clover, wild begonia, dandelion—sprinkling the hillside.

On a spur of the hill stood the ruins of an old brewery. The roof had long since disappeared, and the rain had beaten the stone floors smooth and yellow. Some enterprising Englishman had spent a lifetime here, making beer for his thirsty compatriots in the plains. Now, moss and ferns and maidenhair grew from the walls. In a hollow beneath a flight of worn stone steps, a wild cat had made its home. It was a beautiful grey creature, black-striped, with pale green eyes. Sometimes it watched me from the steps or the wall, but it never came near.

No one lived on the hill, except occasionally a coal-burner in a temporary grass-thatched hut. But villagers used the path, grazing their sheep and cattle on the grassy slopes. Each cow or sheep had a bell suspended from its neck, to let the shepherd-boy know of its whereabouts. The boy could then lie in the sun and eat wild strawberries without fear of losing his animals.

I remembered some of the shepherd boys and girls.

There was a boy who played a flute. Its rough, sweet, straightforward notes travelled clearly across the mountain air. He would greet me with a nod of his head, without taking the flute from his lips. There was a girl who was nearly always cutting grass for fodder. She wore heavy bangles on her feet, and long silver earrings. She did not speak much either, but she always had a wide grin on her face when she met me on the path. She used to sing to herself, or to the sheep, to the grass, or to the sickle in her hand.

And there was a boy who carried milk into town (a distance of about five miles), who would often fall into step with me, to hold a long conversation. He had never been away from the hills, or in a large city. He had never been in a train. I told him about the cities, and he told me about his village; how they make bread from maize, how fish were to be caught in the mountain streams, how the bears came to steal his father's pumpkins. Whenever the pumpkins were ripe, he told me, the bears would come and carry them off.

These things I remembered—these, and the smell of pine needles, the silver of oak-leaves and the red of maple, the call of the Himalayan cuckoo, and the mist, like a wet face-cloth, pressing against the hills.

Odd, how some little incident, some snatch of conversation, comes back to one again and again, in the most unlikely places. Standing in the aisle of a crowded tube train on a Monday morning, my nose tucked into the back page of someone else's newspaper, I suddenly had a vision of a bear making off with a ripe pumpkin.

A bear and a pumpkin—and there, between Goodge Street and Tottenham Court Road stations, all the smells and sounds of the Himalayas came rushing back to me.

❅

Lost all my money

I've lost all my money,
And I'm on my way home;
Home to the hills and a field of rocks.
Nothing in the city but a sickness of the soul,
Nothing to earn but sorrow . . . .
I've lost all my money
And I'm on my way home,
With nothing to buy my way home . . . .
I've lost all my money
And I can't bribe the guard,
So help me, O Lord,
On my way home . . . .

A Mountain Stream

THERE IS A brook at the bottom of the hill. From where I live I can always hear its murmur, but I am no longer conscious of the sound except when I return from a trip to the plains.

And yet I have grown so used to the constant music of water that when I leave it behind I feel naked and alone, bereft of my moorings. It is like getting accustomed to the friendly rattle of teacups every morning, and then waking one day to a deathly stillness and a fleeting moment of panic.

Below the house is a forest of oak and maple and rhododendron. A path twists its way down through the trees over an open ridge where red sorrel grows wild and then down steeply through a tangle of thorn bushes, creepers and rangal-bamboo.

At the bottom of the hill the path leads on to a grassy verge, surrounded by wild rose. The stream runs close by the verge, tumbling over smooth pebbles over rocks worn yellow with age on its way to the plains and to the little Song river and finally to the sacred Ganga.

When I first discovered the stream it was April and the wild roses were flowering, small white blossoms lying in clusters. There were still pink and blue primroses on the hill-slopes and an occasional late-flowering rhododendron provided a splash of red against the dark green of the hill.

A spotted forktail, a bird of the Himalayan streams, was much in evidence during those early visits. It moved nimbly over the boulders with a fairy tread and continually wagged its tail. Both of us had a fondness for standing in running water. Once, while I stood in the stream, I saw a snake swim past, a slim brown snake, beautiful and lonely. A snake in water is a lovely creature.

In May and June, when the hills are always brown and dry, it remained cool and green near the stream where ferns and maidenhair and long grasses continued to thrive. Downstream, I found a small pool where I could bathe and a cave with water dripping from the roof, the water spangled gold and silver in the shafts of sunlight that pushed through the slits in the cave-roof.

Few people came here. Sometimes a milkman or a coal-burner would cross the stream on his way to a village; but the nearby hill-station's summer visitors had not discovered this haven of wild and green things.

The monkeys—langurs with white and silver-grey fur, black faces and long swishing tails—had discovered the place but they kept to the trees and sunlit slopes. They grew quite accustomed to my presence and carried on about their work and play as though I did not exist.

The young ones scuffled and wrestled like boys while their parents attended to each others toilets, stretching themselves out on the grass, beautiful animals with slim waists and long sinewy legs and tails full of character. They were clean and polite, much nicer than the red monkeys of the plains.

During the rains the stream became a rushing torrent, bushes and small trees were swept away and the friendly murmur of the water became a threatening boom. I did not visit the place too often. There were leeches in the long grass and they would fasten themselves onto my legs and feast on my blood.

But it was always worthwhile tramping through the forest to feast my eyes on the foliage that sprang up in tropical profusion—soft, spongy moss; great stag-fern on the trunks of trees; mysterious and sometimes evil-looking lilies and orchids, wild dahlias and the climbing convolvulus opening its purple secrets to the morning sun.

And when the rains were over and it was October and the birds were in song again. I could lie in the sun on sweet-smelling grass and gaze up through a pattern of oak leaves into a blind-blue heaven. And I would thank my God for leaves and grass and the smell of things, the smell of mint and myrtle and bruised clover, and the touch of things, the touch of grass and air and sky, the touch of the sky's blueness.

And then after a November hail-storm it was winter and I could not lie on the frost-bitten grass. The sound of the stream was the same but I missed the birds; and the grey skies came clutching at my heart and the rain and sleet drove me indoors.

It snowed—the snow lay heavy on the branches of the oak trees and piled up in the culverts—and the grass and the ferns and wild flowers were pressed to sleep beneath a cold white blanket: but the stream flowed on, pushing its way through and under the whiteness, towards another river, towards another spring.

A Lime Tree in the Hills

I WAKE TO what sounds like the din of a factory buzzer but is in fact the music of a single vociferous cicada in the lime tree near my bed.

We have slept out of doors. I wake at first light, focus on a pattern of small, glossy leaves, and then through them see the mountains, the mighty Himalayas, striding away into an immensity of sky.

'In a thousand ages of the gods I could not tell thee of the glories of Himachal.' So a poet confessed at the dawn of Indian history, and no one since has been able to do real justice to the Himalayas. We have climbed their highest peaks, but still the mountains remain remote, mysterious, primeval.

No wonder, then, that the people who live on these mountain slopes, in the mist-filled valleys of Garhwal, have long since learned humility, patience, and a quiet reserve.

*

I am their guest for a few days. My friend, Gajadhar, has brought me to his home, to his village above the little Nayar river. We took a train up to the foothills and then we took a bus, and when we were in the hills we walked until we came to this village called Manjari clinging to the terraced slopes of a very proud, very permanent mountain.

It is my fourth morning in the village. Other mornings I was waked by the throaty chuckles of the redbilled blue magpies, but today the cicada has drowned all birdsong.

Early though it is, I am the last to get up. Gajadhar is exercising in the courtyard. He has a fine physique, with the sturdy legs that most Garhwalis possess. I am sure he will realize his ambition of getting into the army. His younger brother, Chakradhar, a slim fair youth, is milking the family's buffalo. Their mother is lighting a fire. She is a handsome woman, although her ears, weighed down by heavy silver earrings, have lost their natural shape. The smaller children, a boy and a girl, are getting ready for school. Their father is in the army, and he is away for most of the year. Gajadhar has been going to a college in the plains; but his mother, with the help of Chakradhar, manages to look after the fields, the house, the goats, and the buffalo. There are spring sowings of corn; monsoon ploughings; September harvestings of rice, and then again autumn sowings of wheat and barley.

They depend on rainfall here, as the village is far above the river. The monsoon is still a month away, but there must be water for cooking, washing, and drinking, and this has to be fetched from the river. And so, after a glass each of hot buffalo's milk, the two brothers and I set off down a rough track to the river.

*

The sun has climbed the mountains but it has yet to reach the narrow valley. We bathe in the river. Gajadhar and Chakradhar dive in off a massive rock; but I wade in circumspectly, unfamiliar with the river's depth and currents. The water, a milky blue, has come from the melting snows and is very cold. I bathe quickly and then dash for a strip of sand where a little sunshine has now spilt down the mountain in warm, golden pools of light.

A little later, buckets filled, we toil up the steep mountainside. A different way this time. We have to take the proper path if we are not to come tumbling down with our pails of water. The path leads up past the school, a small temple, and a single shop in which it is possible to buy soap, salt, and a few other necessities. It is also the post office.

The postman has yet to arrive. The mail is brought in relays from Lansdowne, about thirty miles distant. The Manjari postman, who has to cover eight miles and deliver letters at several small villages on the route, should arrive around noon. He also serves as a newspaper, bringing the village people, news of the outside world. Over the years he has acquired a reputation for being highly inventive and sometimes creating his own news; so much so that when he told the villagers that men had landed on the moon no one believed him. There are still a few sceptics.

*

Gajadhar has been walking out of the village almost every day, anxious for a letter. He is expecting the result of his army entrance exam. If he is successful, he will be called for an interview. And then, if he makes a good impression, he will be given training as an officer cadet. After two years he will be a 2nd lieutenant! His father, after twelve years in the army, is only a corporal. But his father never went to school. There were no schools in the hills in those days.

As we pass the small village school, the children, who have been having a break, crowd round us, eager to have a glimpse of me. They have never seen a white face before. The adults had dealt with British officials in the Forties but it is over twenty years since a European stepped into the village. I am the cynosure of all eyes. The children exclaim, point at me with delight, chatter among themselves. I might be a visitor from another planet instead of just an itinerant writer from the plains.

For Gajadhar, the day is a trial of his patience. First we hear that there has been a landslide and that the postman cannot reach us. Then we hear that, although there was a landslide, the postman had already passed the spot in safety. Another alarming rumour has it that the postman disappeared with the landslide! This is soon denied. The postman is safe. It was only the mailbag that disappeared!

*

And then, at two in the afternoon, the postman turns up. He tells us that there was indeed a landslide but that it took place

on someone else's route. A mischievous urchin who passed
him on the way was apparently responsible for all the rumours.
But we suspect the postman of having something to do with
them.

Yes, Gajadhar has passed his exam and will leave with me
in the morning. We have to be up early to complete the thirty-
mile trek in a single day. And so, after an evening with friends,
and a partridge for dinner (a present from a neighbour who
thinks Gajadhar will make a fine husband for his comely
daughter), we retire to our beds: I, to my cot under the lime
tree. The moon has not yet risen and the cicadas are silent.

I stretch myself out on the cot under a sky brilliant with
stars. And as I close my eyes someone brushes against the lime
tree, bruising its leaves; and the good fresh fragrance of lime
comes to me on the night air, making that moment memorable
for all time.

A New Flower

It was the first day of spring (according to the Hindu calendar), but here in the Himalayas it still seemed mid-winter. A cold wind hummed and whistled through the pines, while dark rain-clouds were swept along by the west wind only to be thrust back by the east wind.

I was climbing the steep road to my cottage at the top of the hill when I was overtaken by nine-year old Usha hurrying back from school. She had tied a scarf round her head to keep her hair from blowing about. Dark hair and eyes, and pink cheeks, were all accentuated by the patches of snow still lying on the hillside.

'Look,' she said, pointing. 'A new flower!' It was a single, butter-yellow blossom, and it stood out like a bright star against the drab winter grass. I hadn't seen anything like it before, and had no idea what its name might be. No doubt its existence was recorded in some botanical tome. But for me it was a discovery.

'Shall I pick it for you?' asked Usha. 'No, don't,' I said. 'It may be the only one. If we break it, there may not be any more. Let's leave it there and see if it seeds.' We scrambled up the slope and examined the flower more closely. It was very delicate and soft-petalled looking as though it might fall at any moment.

'It will be finished if it rains,' said Usha. And it did rain that night—rain mingled with sleet and hail. It rattled and swished on the corrugated tin roof; but in the morning the sun came out. I walked up the road without really expecting to see the flower again. And Usha had been right. The flower had disappeared in the storm. But two other buds, unnoticed by us the day before, had opened. It was as though two tiny stars had fallen to earth in the night.

I did not see Usha that day; but the following day, when we met on the road, I showed her the fresh blossoms. And they were still there, two days later, when I passed by; but so were two goats, grazing on the short grass and thorny thickets of the slope. I had no idea if they were partial to these particular flowers, but I did know that goats would eat almost anything and I was taking no chances.

Scrambling up the steep slope, I began to shoo them away. One goat retreated; but the other lowered his horns, gave me a baleful look, and refused to move. It reminded me a little of my grandfather's pet goat who had once pushed a visiting official into a bed of nasturtiums; so I allowed discretion to be the better part of valour, and backed away.

Just then, Usha came along and, sizing up the situation, came to the rescue. She unfurled her pretty blue umbrella and advanced on the goat shouting at it in goat language. (She had her own goats at home.) The beast retreated, and the flowers (and my own dignity) were saved.

As the days grew warmer, the flowers faded and finally disappeared. I forgot all about them, and so did Usha. There were lessons and exams for her to worry about, and rent and electricity bills to occupy a freelance writer's thoughts.

The months passed, summer and autumn came and went, with their own more showy blooms; and in no time at all, winter returned with cold winds blowing from all directions.

One day I heard Usha calling to me from the hillside. I looked up and saw her standing behind a little cluster of golden star-shaped flowers—not, perhaps, as spectacular as Wordsworth's field of golden daffodils but, all the same, an enchanting sight for one who had played a small part in perpetuating their existence.

Where there had been one flowering plant, there were now several. Usha and I speculated on the prospect of the entire hillside being covered with the flowers in a few years' time.

I still do not know the botanical name for the little flower. I can't remember long Latin names anyway. But Usha tells me that she has seen it growing near her father's village, on the next mountain, and that the hill people call it 'Basant', which means spring.

Although I am just a little disappointed that we are not, after all, the discoverers of a new species, this is outweighed by our pleasure in knowing that the flower flourishes in other places. May it multiply!

The Joy of Water

Each drop represents a little bit of creation—and of life itself.

When the monsoon brings to northern India the first rains of summer, the parched earth opens its pores and quenches its thirst with a hiss of ecstasy. After baking in the sun for the last few months, the land looks cracked, dusty and tired. Now, almost overnight, new grass springs up, there is renewal everywhere, and the damp earth releases a fragrance sweeter than any devised by man.

Water brings joy to earth, grass, leaf-bud, blossom, insect, bird, animal and the pounding heart of man. Small children run out of their homes to romp naked in the rain. Buffaloes, which have spent the summer listlessly around lakes gone dry, now plunge into a heaven of muddy water. Soon the lakes and rivers will overflow with the monsoon's generosity.

Trekking in the Himalayan foothills, I recently walked for kilometres without encountering habitation. I was just scolding myself for not having brought along a water bottle, when I came across a patch of green on a rock face. I parted a curtain of tender maidenhair fern and discovered a tiny spring issuing from the rock—nectar for the thirsty traveller.

I stayed there for hours, watching the water descend, drop by drop, into a tiny casement in the rocks. Each drop reflected creation. That same spring, I later discovered, joined other springs to form a swift, tumbling stream, which went cascading down the hill into other streams until, in the plains, it became part of a river. And that river flowed into another mightier river that kilometres later emptied into the ocean. Be like water, taught Lao-tzu, philosopher and founder of Taoism. Soft and limpid, it finds its way through, over or under any obstacle. It does not quarrel; it simply moves on.

A small pool in the rocks outside my cottage in the Mussoorie hills, provides me endless delight. Water beetles paddle the surface, while tiny fish lurk in the shallows. Sometimes a spotted fork-tail comes to drink, hopping delicately from rock to rock. And once I saw a barking deer, head lowered at the edge of the pool. I stood very still, anxious that it should drink its fill. It did, and then, looking up, saw me and leapt across the ravine to disappear into the forest.

In summer the pool is almost dry. Even this morning, there was just enough water for the fish and tadpoles to survive. But as I write, there is a pattering on the tin roof of the cottage, and I look out to see the raindrops pitting the surface of the pool.

Tomorrow the spotted fork-tail will be back. Perhaps the barking deer will return. I open the window wide and allow the fragrance of the rain and freshened earth to waft into my room.

Rain

After weeks of heat and dust
How welcome is the rain.
It washes the leaves,
Gives new life to grass,
Draws out the scent of the earth.
It rattles on the roof,
Gurgles along the drainpipe
Collects in a puddle in the middle of the lawn—
The birds come to bathe.

When the sun comes out
A lizard crawls up from a crack in a rock.
'Small brown lizard
Basking in the sun
You too have your life to live
Your race to run.'

At night we look through the branches
of the cherry tree.
The sky is rain-washed, star-bright.

Sounds I Like to Hear

ALL NIGHT THE rain has been drumming on the corrugated tin roof. There has been no storm, no thunder just the steady swish of a tropical downpour. It helps one to lie awake; at the same time, it doesn't keep one from sleeping.

It is a good sound to read by—the rain outside, the quiet within—and, although tin roofs are given to springing unaccountable leaks, there is in general a feeling of being untouched by, and yet in touch with, the rain.

Gentle rain on a tin roof is one of my favourite sounds. And early in the morning, when the rain has stopped, there are other sounds I like to hear—a crow shaking the raindrops from his feathers and cawing rather disconsolately; babblers and bulbuls bustling in and out of bushes and long grass in search of worms and insects; the sweet, ascending trill of the Himalayan whistling-thrush; dogs rushing through damp undergrowth.

A cherry tree, bowed down by the heavy rain, suddenly rights itself, flinging pellets of water in my face.

Some of the best sounds are made by water. The water of a mountain stream, always in a hurry, bubbling over rocks and chattering, 'I'm late, I'm late!' like the White Rabbit, tumbling over itself in its anxiety to reach the bottom of the hill, the sound of the sea, especially when it is far away—or when you hear it by putting a sea shell to your ear. The sound made by dry and thirsty earth, as it sucks at a sprinkling of water. Or the sound of a child drinking thirstily the water running down his chin and throat.

Water gushing out of the pans of an old well outside a village while a camel moves silently round the well. Bullock-cart wheels creaking over rough country roads. The clip-clop of a pony carriage, and the tinkle of its bell,

and the singsong call of its driver . . . .

Bells in the hills. A schoolbell ringing, and children's voices drifting through an open window. A temple-bell, heard faintly from across the valley. Heavy silver ankle-bells on the feet of sturdy hill women. Sheep bells heard high up on the mountainside.

Do falling petals make a sound? Just the tiniest and softest of sounds, like the drift of falling snow. Of course big flowers, like dahlias, drop their petals with a very definite flop. These are showoffs, like the hawk-moth who comes flapping into the rooms at night instead of emulating the butterfly dipping lazily on the afternoon breeze.

*

One must return to the birds for favourite sounds, and the birds of the plains differ from the birds of the hills. On a cold winter morning in the plains of northern India, if you walk some way into the jungle you will hear the familiar call of the black partridge: *Bhagwan teri qudrat* it seems to cry, which means: 'Oh God! Great is thy might.'

The cry rises from the bushes in all directions; but an hour later not a bird is to be seen or heard and the jungle is so very still that the silence seems to shout at you.

There are sounds that come from a distance, beautiful because they are far away, voices on the wind—they 'walketh upon the wings of the wind'. The cries of fishermen out on the river. Drums beating rhythmically in a distant village. The croaking of frogs from the rainwater pond behind the house. I mean frogs at a distance. A frog croaking beneath one's window is as welcome as a motor horn.

But some people like motor horns. I know a taxi-driver who never misses an opportunity to use his horn. It was made to his own specifications, and it gives out a resonant bugle-call. He never tires of using it. Cyclists and pedestrians always scatter at his approach. Other cars veer off the road. He is proud of his horn. He loves its strident sound—which only goes to show that some men's sounds are other men's noises!

Homely sounds, though we don't often think about them, are the ones we miss most when they are gone. A kettle on the boil. A door that creaks on its hinges. Old sofa springs. Familiar voices lighting up the dark. Ducks quacking in the rain.

And so we return to the rain, with which my favourite sounds began.

I have sat out in the open at night, after a shower of rain when the whole air is murmuring and tinkling with the voices of crickets and grasshoppers and little frogs. There is one melodious sound, a sweet repeated trill, which I have never been able to trace to its source. Perhaps it is a little tree frog. Or it may be a small green cricket. I shall never know.

I am not sure that I really want to know. In an age when a scientific and rational explanation has been given for almost everything we see and touch and hear, it is good to be left with one small mystery, a mystery sweet and satisfying and entirely my own.

❄

Listen!

Listen to the night wind in the trees,
Listen to the summer grass singing;
Listen to the time that's tripping by,
And the dawn dew falling.
Listen to the moon as it climbs the sky,
Listen to the pebbles humming;
Listen to the mist in the trembling leaves,
And the silence calling.

Dragon in the Tunnel

THE FIRST TIME I saw a train, I was standing on a wooded slope outside a tunnel, not far from Kalka. Suddenly, with a shrill whistle and great burst of steam, a green and black engine came snorting out of the blackness.

I turned and ran to my father. 'A dragon!' I shouted. 'There's a dragon coming out of its cave!'

Since then, steam engines and dragons have always inspired the same sort of feelings in me—wonder and awe and delight. I would like to see a real dragon one day, green and gold and—because I have always preferred the 'reluctant' sort—rather shy and gentle; but until that day comes, I shall be content with steam engines.

In India the steam engine is still very much with us. In 1855 the East India Railway was opened between Calcutta and Raniganj, a distance of 122 miles. By the turn of the century, India had one of the most extensive railway systems in the world. Today, the hundreds of trains that criss-cross the subcontinent, panting over the desert and plain, through hill and forest, are still pulled by these snorting monsters who belch smoke by day and scatter red stars in the night.

Even now, when I see a train coming round the bend of a hill, on crossing a bridge, or cutting across a wide flat plain, I feel the same sort of innocent wonder that I felt as a boy. Where are all these people going to, and where have they come from, and what are they really like? When children wave to me from carriage windows I wave back to them. It is a habit I have never lost. And sometimes I am in a train, waving, and the children from the nearby villages come running out of their mud huts to wave back to me—well, not to me exactly, it is really the train they are waving to . . . .

Small wayside stations have always fascinated me. Manned sometimes by just one or two railway employees, and often situated in the middle of a damp subtropical forest, or clinging to the mountainside on the way to Simla or Darjeeling, these little stations are, for me, outposts of romance, lonely symbols of the pioneering spirit that led men to lay tracks into the remote corners of the earth.

I remember such a stop on a line that went through the Terai forests near the foothills of the Himalayas. At about ten at night, the *khilasi*, or station watchman, lit his kerosene lamp and started walking up the tracks into the jungle.

'Where are you going?' I asked.

'To see if the tunnel is clear,' he said. 'The Overland Mail comes in twenty minutes.'

I accompanied him a furlong or two along the track, through a deep cutting which led to the tunnel. Every night, the *khilasi* walked through the dark tunnel, and then stood outside to wave his lamp to the oncoming train as a signal that the track was clear. If the engine driver did not see the lamp he stopped the train. It always slowed down near the cutting.

Having inspected the tunnel, we stood outside, waiting for the train. It seemed a long time coming. There was no moon, and the dense forest seemed to be trying to crowd us into the narrow cutting. The sounds of the forest came to us—the belling of a sambhur deer and the cry of a jackal told us that perhaps a tiger or a leopard was on the prowl. There were strange, nocturnal bird sounds; and then silence.

The *khilasi* stood outside the tunnel, trimming his lamp, listening to the faint sounds of the jungle—sounds which only he could identify and understand. Something made him stand very still for a few moments, peering into the darkness, and I knew that everything was not as it should be.

'There is something in the tunnel,' he said.

I could hear nothing at first, but then there came a regular sawing sound, just like the sound made by someone sawing through the branch of a tree.

'Baghera!' whispered the *khilasi*. He had said enough to enable me to recognize the sound—the sawing of a leopard trying to find its mate. 'The train will be coming soon. We must drive the animal out, or it will be run over!'

He must have sensed my surprise, because he said, 'Do not be afraid . . . . I know this leopard well. We have seen each other many times. He has a weakness for stray dogs and goats, but he will not harm us.' He gave me his small handaxe to hold and, raising his lamp high, started walking into the tunnel, shouting at the top of his voice to try and scare away the animal. I followed close behind him.

We had gone about twenty yards into the tunnel when the light from the lamp fell on the leopard, which was crouching between the tracks, only about twenty feet away from us. It bared its teeth in a snarl and went down on its stomach, tail twisting. I thought it was going to spring. The *khilasi* and I both shouted together. Our voices rang and echoed through the tunnel. And the leopard, uncertain as to how many humans were in there with him, turned swiftly and disappeared into the darkness ahead.

The *khilasi* and I walked on till the end of the tunnel without seeing the leopard again. As we returned to the entrance of the tunnel the rails began to hum and we knew the train was coming.

I put my hand to one of the rails and felt its tremor. And then the engine came round the bend, hissing at us, scattering sparks into the darkness, defying the jungle as it roared through the steep sides of the cutting. It charged straight at the tunnel and into it, thundering past us like the beautiful dragon of my dreams.

And when it had gone, the silence returned and the forest breathed again. Only the rails still trembled with the passing of the train.

As a Boy

As a boy I stood on the edge of the railway-cutting,
Outside the dark tunnel, my hands touching
The hot rails, waiting for them to tremble
At the coming of the noonday train.
The whistle of the engine hung on the forest's silence.
Then out of the tunnel, a green-gold dragon
Came plunging, thundering past—
Out of the tunnel, out of the dark.

And the train rolled on, every day
Hundreds of people coming or going or running away—
Goodbye, goodbye !
I haven't seen you again, bright boy at the carriage window,
Waving to me, calling,
But I've loved you all these years and looked for you
everywhere,
In cities and villages, beside the sea,
In the mountains, in crowds at distant places;
Returning always to the forest's silence,
To watch the windows of some passing train . . . .

Hill of the Fairies

Fairy Hill, or Pari Tibba as the paharis call it, is a lonely uninhabited mountain lying to the east of Mussoorie, at a height of about 6,000 feet. I have visited it occasionally, scrambling up its rocky slopes where the only paths are the narrow tracks made by goats and the small hill cattle. Rhododendrons and a few stunted oaks are the only trees on the hillsides, but at the summit is a small, grassy plateau ringed by pine trees.

It may have been on this plateau that the early settlers tried building their houses. All their attempts met with failure. The area seemed to attract the worst of any thunderstorm, and several dwellings were struck by lightning and burnt to the ground. People then confined themselves to the adjacent Landour hill, where a flourishing hill-station soon grew up.

Why Pari Tibba should be struck so often by lightning has always been something of a mystery to me. Its soil and rock seem no different from the soil or rock of any other mountain in the vicinity. Perhaps a geologist can explain the phenomenon; or perhaps it has something to do with the fairies.

'Why do they call it the Hill of the Fairies?' I asked an old resident, a retired schoolteacher. 'Is the place haunted?'

'So they say,' he said.

'Who say?'

'Oh, people who have heard it's haunted. Some years after the site was abandoned by the settlers, two young runaway lovers took shelter for the night in one of the ruins. There was a bad storm and they were struck by lightning. Their charred bodies were found a few days later. They came from different communities and were buried far from each other, but their spirits hold a tryst every night under the pine trees. You might see them if you're on Pari Tibba after sunset.'

There are no ruins on Pari Tibba, and I can only presume that the building materials were taken away for use elsewhere. And I did not stay on the hill till after sunset. Had I tried climbing downhill in the dark, I would probably have ended up as the third ghost on the mountain. The lovers might have resented my intrusion; or, who knows, they might have welcomed a change. After a hundred years together on a wind-swept mountain-top, even the most ardent of lovers must tire of each other.

Who could have been seeing ghosts on Pari Tibba after sunset? The nearest resident is a woodcutter who makes charcoal at the bottom of the hill. Terraced fields and a small village straddle the next hill. But the only inhabitants of Pari Tibba are the langurs. They feed on oak leaves and rhododendron buds. The rhododendrons contain an intoxicating nectar, and after dining—or wining—to excess, the young monkeys tumble about on the grass in high spirits.

The black bulbuls also feed on the nectar of the rhododendron flower, and perhaps this accounts for the cheekiness of these birds. They are aggressive, disreputable little creatures, who go about in rowdy gangs. The song of most bulbuls consists of several pleasant tinkling notes; but that of the Himalayan black bulbul is as musical as the bray of an ass. Men of science, in their wisdom, have given this bird the sibilant name of *Hypsipetes psaroides*. But the hillmen, in their greater wisdom, call the species the *ban bakra*, which means the 'jungle goat'.

Perhaps the flowers have something to do with the fairy legend. In April and May, Pari Tibba is covered with the dazzling yellow flowers of St. John's Wort (wort meaning herb). The paharis call the flower a wild rose, and it does resemble one. In Ireland it is called the Rose of Sharon.

In Europe this flower is reputed to possess certain magical and curative properties. It is believed to drive away all evil and protect you from witches. But do not tread on St. John's Wort after sunset, lest a fairy horseman come and carry you off, landing you almost anywhere.

By day, St. John's Wort is kindly. Are you insane? Then

drink the sap from the leaves of the plant, and you will be cured. Are you hurt? Take the juice and apply it to your wound—and if at first this doesn't help, just keep applying juice until you stop bleeding, or breathing. Are you bald? Then rise early and bathe your head with the dew from St. John's Wort, and your hair will grow again—if you don't catch pneumonia.

Can St. John's Wort be connected with the fairy legend of Pari Tibba? It is said that most flowers, when they die, become fairies. This might be especially true of St. John's Wort.

There is yet another legend connected with the mountain. A shepherd-boy, playing on his flute, discovered a beautiful silver snake basking on a rock. The snake spoke to the boy, saying, 'I was a princess once, but a jealous witch cast a spell over me and turned me into a snake. This spell can only be broken if someone who is pure in heart kisses me thrice. Many years have passed, and I have not been able to find one who is pure in heart.' Then the shepherd-boy took the snake in his arms, and he put his lips to its mouth, and at the third kiss he discovered that he was holding a beautiful princess in his arms. What happened afterwards is anybody's guess.

There are snakes on Pari Tibba, and though they are probably harmless, I have never tried taking one of them in my arms. Once, near a spring, I came upon a checkered water snake. Its body was a series of bulges. I used a stick to exert pressure along the snake's length, and it disgorged five frogs. They came out one after the other, and, to my astonishment, hopped off, little the worse for their harrowing experience. Perhaps they, too, were enchanted. Perhaps shepherd-boys, when they kiss the snake-princess, are turned into frogs and remain inside the snake's belly until a writer comes along with a magic stick and releases them from bondage.

Biologists probably have their own explanation for the frogs, but I'm all for perpetuating the fairy legends of Pari Tibba.

The Open Road

As THE YEARS go by, I do not walk as far or as fast as I
used to; but speed and distance were never my forte. Like
J. Krishnamurti, I believe that the journey is more important
than the destination. But, then, I have never really had a
destination. The glory that comes from conquering the
Himalayan peaks is not for me. My greatest pleasure lies in
taking a path—any old path will do—and following it until it
leads me to a forest-glade or village or stream or windy hilltop.

This sort of tramping (it does not even qualify as trekking)
is a compulsive thing with me. You could call it my vice, since
it is stronger than the desire for wine, women or song. To get
on to the open road fills me with *joie de vivre*, gives me an
exhilaration not found in other, possibly more worthy, pursuits.

Only this afternoon I had one of my more enjoyable tramps.
I had been cooped up in my room for several days, while
outside it rained and hailed and snowed and the wind blew
icily from all directions. It seemed ages since I'd taken a long
walk. Fed up with it all, I pulled on my overcoat, banged the
door shut and set off up the hillside.

I kept to the main road, but because of the heavy snow there
were no vehicles on it. Even as I walked, flurries of snow
struck my face, and collected on my coat and head. Up at the
top of the hill, the deodars were clothed in a mantle of white.
It was fairyland: everything still and silent. The only movement
was the circling of an eagle over the trees. I walked for an
hour, and passed only one person, the milkman on his way
back to his village. His cans were crowned with snow. He
looked a little tipsy. He asked me the time, but before I could
tell him he shook me by the hand and said I was a good fellow
because I never complained about the water in the milk. I told

him that as long as he used clean water, I'd contain my wrath.

On my way back, I passed a small group. It consisted of a person in some sort of uniform (because of the snow I couldn't really make it out), who was hurling epithets at several small children who were busy throwing snowballs at him. He kept shouting: 'Do you know who I am?' Do you know who I am?' The children did not want to know. They were only interested in hitting their target, and succeeded once in every five or six attempts.

I came home exhilarated and immediately sat down beside the stove to write this piece. I found some lines of Stevenson's which seemed appropriate:

> *And this shall be for music when no one else is near,*
> *The fine song for singing, the rare song to hear!*
> *That only I remember, that only you admire,*
> *Of the broad road that stretches, and the roadside fire.*

He speaks directly to me, across the mists of time: R. L. Stevenson, prince of essayists. There is none like him today. We hurry, hurry in a heat of hope—and who has time for roadside fires, except, perhaps, those who must work on the roads in all weathers?

Whenever I walk into the hills, I come across gangs of road-workers breaking stones, cutting into the rocky hillsides, building retaining walls. I am not against more roads—especially in the hills, where the people have remained impoverished largely because of the inaccessibility of their villages. Besides, a new road is one more road for me to explore, and in the interests of progress I am prepared to put up with the dust raised by the occasional bus. And if it becomes too dusty, one can always leave the main road. There is no dearth of paths leading off into the valleys.

On one such diversionary walk, I reached a village where I was given a drink of curds and a meal of rice and beans. That is another of the attractions of tramping to nowhere in particular—the finding of somewhere in particular; the striking up of friendships; the discovery of new springs and waterfalls, unusual plants, rare flowers, strange birds. In the hills, a new vista opens up at every bend in the road.

That is what makes me a compulsive walker—new vistas, and the charm of the unexpected.

A Quiet Mind

Lord, give me a quiet mind,
That I might listen;
A gentle tone of voice,
That I might comfort others;
A sound and healthy body,
That I might share
In the joy of walking
And leaping and running;
And a good sense of direction
So I might know just where I'm going!

These I Have Loved

SEA SHELLS. THEY are among my earliest memories. I was five years old, walking barefoot along the golden sands of a Kathiawar beach, collecting shells and cowries and taking them home to fill up an old trunk. Some of those shells remained with me through the years, and I still have one. Whenever I put it to my ear, I can listen to the distant music of the Arabian Sea.

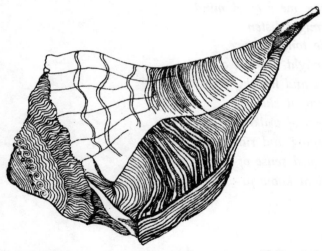

A jack-fruit tree. It stood outside my grandfather's house in Dehradun: it was easy to climb and was generous with its shade; and in its trunk was a large hole where I kept my marbles, sweets, prohibited books and other treasures.

I have always liked the smell of certain leaves, perhaps even more than the scent of flowers. Crushed geranium and chrysanthemum leaves, mint and myrtle, lime and neem trees after rain, and the leaves of ginger, marigolds and nasturtiums.

Of course there were other smells which, as a boy, I especially liked—the smell of pillau and kofta curry, hot jalebis, roast chicken and fried prawns. But these are smells loved by most gourmets (and most boys), and are not as personal as the smell of leaves and grass.

I have always liked trains and railway-stations. I like eating at railway-stations—hot gram, peanuts, puris, oranges . . . .

As a boy, I travelled to Simla in the little train that crawls round and through the mountains. In March the flowers on the rhododendron trees provided splashes of red against the dark green of the hills. Sometimes there would be snow on the ground to add to the contrast.

What else do I love and remember of the hills? Smells, again . . . . The smells of fallen pine-needles, cowdung smoke, spring rain, bruised grass, the pure cold water of mountain streams, the depth and blueness of the sky.

In the hills, I have loved forests. In the plains, I have loved single trees. A lone tree on wide flat plain—even if it is a thin, crooked, nondescript tree—gains beauty and nobility from its isolation, from the precarious nature of its existence.

Of course, I have had my favourites among trees. The banyan, with its great branches spreading to form roots and intricate passageways. The peepul, with its beautiful heart-shaped leaf catching the breeze and fluttering even on the stillest of days. It is always cool under the peepul. The jacaranda and the gulmohur bursting into blossom with the coming of summer. The cherries, peaches and apricots flowering in the hills; the tall handsome chestnuts and the whispering deodars.

Deodars have often inspired me to poetry. One day I wrote:

Trees of God, we call them;
Planted here when the world was young,
The first trees
Their fingers pointing to the stars,
Older than the cedars of Lebanon.

Several of these trees were cut down recently, and I was furious:

> *They cut them down last spring*
> *With swift efficient tools,*
> *The sap was rising still.*
> *The trees bled,*
> *Slaughtered*
> *To make furniture for fools.*

And which flower is most redolent of India, of the heat and light and colour of India? Not for me the lotus or the water-lily, but the single marigold, fresh, golden, dew-drenched, kissed by the morning sun.

The smell of the sea . . . . I lived with it for over a year in the Channel Islands. I liked the sea-mist and I liked the fierce gales that swept across the islands in the winter.

Later, there were the fogs of London; I did not like them, but they made me think of Dickens, and I walked to Wapping and the East India Dock Road, and watched the barges on the Thames. It had my favourite pub, and my favourite fish-and-chips shop.

There were always children flying kites from Primrose Hill or sailing boats in the ponds of Hampstead Heath.

Once we visited the gardens at Kew, and in a hothouse, moist and smelling of the tropics, I remembered the East and some of the simple things I had known—a field of wheat, a stack of sugarcane, a cow at rest and a boy sleeping in the shade of a long, red fingered poinsettia . . . . And I knew I would go home to India.

A Dream of Gardens

A̲s̲ ̲w̲i̲t̲h̲ ̲m̲a̲n̲y̲ who love gardens, I have never really had enough space in which to create a garden of my own. A few square feet of rocky hillside has been the largest patch at my disposal. All that I managed to grow on it were daisies—and they'd probably have grown there anyway. Still, they made for a charmingly dappled hillside throughout the summer, especially on full moon nights when the flowers were at their most radiant.

For the past few years, here in Mussoorie, I have had to live in two small rooms on the third floor of a tumbledown building which has no garden space at all. All the same, it has a number of ever-widening cracks in which wild sorrel, dandelions, thorn-apples and nettles all take root and thrive. You could, I suppose, call it a wild wall-garden. Not that I am deprived of flowers. I am better off than most city-dwellers because I have only to walk a short way out of the hill-station to see (or discover) a variety of flowers in their wild state; and wild flowers are rewarding, because the best ones are often the most difficult to find.

But I have always had this dream of possessing a garden of my own. Not a very formal garden—certainly not the 'stately home' type, with its pools and fountains and neat hedges as described in such detail by Bacon in his essay 'Of Gardens'. Bacon had a methodical mind, and he wanted a methodical garden. I like a garden to be a little untidy, unplanned, full of surprises—rather like my own muddled mind, which gives even me a few surprises at times.

My grandmother's garden in Dehra, in north India, for example; Grandmother liked flowers, and she didn't waste space on lawns and hedges. There was plenty of space at the back of the house for shrubs and fruit trees, but the front garden was a maze of flower-beds of all shapes and sizes, and everything that could grow in Dehra (a fertile valley) was grown in them—masses of sweet peas, petunias, antirrhinum, poppies, phlox, and larkspur, scarlet poinsettia leaves draped the garden walls, while purple and red bougainvillaea climbed the porch; geraniums of many hues mounted the veranda steps; and, indoors, vases full of cut flowers gave the rooms a heady fragrance. I suppose it was this garden of my childhood that implanted in my mind the permanent vision of a perfect garden so that, whenever I am worried or down in the dumps, I close my eyes and conjure up a picture of this lovely place, where I am wandering through forests of cosmos and banks of rambling roses. It does help to soothe an agitated mind. I wouldn't call it meditation. Contemplation, rather.

I remember an aunt who sometimes came to stay with my grandmother, and who had an obsession about watering the flowers. She would be at it morning and evening, an old and rather lopsided watering-can in her frail hands. To everyone's amazement, she would water the garden in all weathers, even during the rains.

'But it's just been raining, aunt,' I would remonstrate. 'Why are you watering the garden?'

'The rain comes from above,' she would reply. 'This is from me. They expect me at this time, you know.'

Grandmother died when I was still a boy, and the garden soon passed into other hands. I've never done well enough to be able to acquire something like it. And there's no point in getting sentimental about the past.

Yes, I'd love to have a garden of my own—spacious and gracious, and full of everything that's fragrant and flowering. But if I don't succeed, never mind—I've still got the dream.

There are in my Garden

There are in my garden

the burnt bronze petals
of shattered marigolds

spears of goldenrod
bending to the load
of pillaging bees

two armoured lizards
a map butterfly
and a division of ants . . . .

A small yellow bird
attacks the last wild cherry blossom
and a laughing boy
stands over new grown clover
where, last year September,
I buried my revolver
in the dark . . . .

A Sweet Savour

I WOULD BE the last person to belittle a flower because of its colour or appearance, but it does happen that my own favourites are those with their own distinctive fragrance.

The rose, of course, is a joy to all—even to my baby granddaughter, who enjoys taking one apart, petal by petal—but there are other, less spectacular blooms, which have a lovely and sometimes elusive fragrance all their own.

I have a special fondness for antirrhinums, or snapdragons, as they are more commonly known. If I sniff hard at them, I don't catch any scent at all. They seem to hold it back from me. But if I walk past a bed of these flowers, or even a single plant, the gentlest of fragrances is wafted to me, zephyr-like. And if I stop to try and take it all in, it has gone again! I find this quite tantalizing, but it has given me a special regard for this modest flower.

Carnations, with their strong scent of cloves, are great show-offs. And here, in India, the jasmine can be rather heady and overpowering. The honeysuckle, too, insists on making its presence known. There is a honeysuckle creeper outside the study window of my cottage in the hills, and all through the summer its sweet, rather cloying fragrance drifts in through the open window. It is delightful at times; but at other times I have to close the window just so that I can give my attention to other, less intrusive, smells—like the soft scent of petunias (another of my favourites) near the doorstep, and pine needles on the hillside, and great bunches of sweet peas placed on my table.

Some flowers can be quite tricky. One would think that the calendula had no scent at all. Certainly the flower gives nothing away. But run your fingers gently over the leaves and then bring them to your face, and you will be touched—just briefly—by the most delicate of aromas.

Sometimes leaves outdo their blooms. The lemon geranium, for instance, is valued more for its fragrant leaves than for its rather indeterminate flowers. It is the same with verbena. And I cannot truthfully say what ordinary mint looks like in flower. The refreshing aroma of its leaves, when crushed, makes up for any absence of floral display.

Not all plants are fragrant. Some, like the asafoetida, will keep strong men at bay. Of course, one man's fragrance might well turn out to be another creature's bad smell. Geraniums, my grandmother insisted, kept snakes away because they couldn't stand the smell of these flowers. She surrounded her north Indian bungalow with pots of geraniums. It's true we never found a snake in the house, so she may have been right!

But snakes must like some smells, close to the gound, or by now they'd have taken to living in more elevated places; but I am told their sense of smell is rather dull. When I lie on summer grass in the Himalayas, I am conscious of the many good smells around me—the grass itself, redolent of the morning's dew; bruised clover; wild violets; tiny buttercups and golden stars and strawberry flowers and many I shall never know the names of . . . .

And the earth itself. It smells differently in different places. But its loveliest fragrance is known only when it receives a shower of rain. And then the scent of wet earth rises as though it were giving something beautiful back to the clouds—a blend of all the fragrant things that grow in it.

Ruskin Bond

Walnut Tree

The walnut tree is the first to lose its leaves,
But at the same time the fruit ripens,
The skin splits, the hard shell of the nut
Stands revealed. Yesterday (the last of August)
You climbed among the last few crumpled leaves,
Slim boy in a walnut tree, your toes
Gripping the tender bark, your fingers
Fondling walnuts, while I waited and counted,
And there were twenty-three walnuts on the grass.
We cracked them open with our teeth.
They were still raw but we could not wait:
The walnuts would age and I might grow younger!

Great Trees I Have Known

LIVING FOR MANY years in a cottage at 7,000 feet in the Garhwal Himalayas, I was fortunate in having a big window that opened out on the forest, so that the trees were almost within my reach. Had I jumped, I should have landed quite safely in the arms of an oak or chestnut.

The incline of the hill was such that my first-floor window opened on what must, I suppose, have been the second-floor. I never made the jump, but the big langurs, silver-red monkeys with long swishing tails, often leapt from the trees onto the corrugated tin roof and made enough noise to disturb the bats sleeping in the space between the roof and ceiling.

Standing on its own was a walnut tree, and truly, this was a tree for all seasons. In winter the branches were bare but they were smooth and straight and round like the arms of a woman in a painting by Jamini Roy. In the spring each branch produced a hard bright spear of new leaf. By midsummer the entire tree was in leaf, and towards the end of the monsoon the walnuts, encased in their green jackets, had reached maturity.

Then the jackets began to split, revealing the hard brown shell of the walnuts. Inside the shell was the nut itself. Look closely at the nut and you will notice that it is shaped rather like the human brain. No wonder the ancients prescribed walnuts for headaches!

Every year the tree gave me a basket of walnuts. But last year the walnuts were disappearing one by one, and I was at a loss to know who had been taking them. Could it have been Biju, the milkman's son? He was an inveterate tree-climber. But he was usually to be found on oak trees, gathering fodder for his cows. He told me that his cows liked oak leaves but did not care for walnuts. He admitted that they had relished my dahlias, which they had eaten the previous week, but he denied having fed them walnuts.

It wasn't the woodpecker. He was out there every day, knocking furiously against the bark of the tree, trying to prise an insect out of a narrow crack. He was strictly non-vegetarian and none the worse for it.

One day I found a fat langur sitting in the walnut tree. I watched him for some time to see if he was going to help himself to the nuts, but he was only sunning himself. When he thought I wasn't looking, he came down and ate the geraniums; but he did not take any walnuts.

The walnuts had been disappearing early in the morning while I was still in bed. So one morning I surprised every one, including myself, by getting up before sunrise. I was just in time to catch the culprit climbing out of the walnut tree.

She was an old woman who sometimes came to cut grass on the hillside. Her face was as wrinkled as the walnuts she had been helping herself to. In spite of her age, her arms and legs were sturdy. When she saw me, she was as swift as a civet-cat in getting out of the tree.

'And how many walnuts did you gather today, Grandmother?' I asked.

'Only two,' she said with a giggle, offering them to me on her open palm. I accepted one of them. Encouraged, she climbed back into the tree and helped herself to the remaining nuts. It was impossible to object. I was taken up in admiration of her agility in the tree. She must have been about sixty, and I was a mere forty-five, but I knew I would never be climbing trees again.

To the victor the spoils!

The horse-chestnuts are inedible, even the monkeys throw them away in disgust. Once, on passing beneath a horse-chestnut tree, a couple of chestnuts bounced off my head. Looking up, I saw that they had been dropped on me by a couple of mischievous rhesus-monkeys.

The tree itself is a friendly one, especially in summer when it is in full leaf. The least breath of wind makes the leaves break into conversation, and their rustle is a cheerful sound, unlike the sad notes of pine trees in the wind. The spring flowers look like candelabra, and when the blossoms fall they carpet the hillside with their pale pink petals.

We pass now to my favourite tree, the deodar. In Garhwal and Kumaon it is called *dujar* or *devdar*, in Jaunsar and in parts of Himachal it is known as the *Kelu kelon*. It is also identified with the cedar of Lebanon (the cones are identical), although the deodar's needles are slightly longer and more bluish. Trees, like humans, change with their environment. Several persons familiar with the deodar at Indian hill-stations, when asked to point it out in London's Kew Gardens, indicated the cedar of Lebanon; and shown a deodar, declared that they had never seen such a tree in the Himalayas!

We shall stick to the name deodar, which comes from the Sanskrit *deva-daru* (divine tree). It is a sacred tree in the Himalayas; not worshipped, nor protected in the way that a peepul is in the plains, but sacred in that its timber has always been used in temples, for doors, windows, walls and even roofs. Quite frankly, I would just as soon worship the deodar as worship anything, for in the beauty and majesty it represents Creation in its most noble aspect.

No one who has lived amongst deodar would deny that it is the most godlike of Himalayan trees. It stands erect, dignified; and though in a strong wind it may hum and sigh and moan, it does not bend to the wind. The snow slips softly from its resilient branches. In the spring the new leaves are a tender green, while during monsoon the tiny young cones spread like blossoms in the dark green folds of the branches. The deodar thrives in the rain and enjoys the company of its own kind. Where one deodar grows, there will be others. Isolate a young tree and it will often pine away.

The great deodar forests are found along the upper reaches of the Bhagirathi valley and the Tons in Garhwal; and in Himachal and Kashmir, along the Chenab and the Jhelum, and also on the Kishenganga; it is at its best between 7,000 and 9,000 feet. I had expected to find it on the upper reaches of the Alakananda, but could not find a single deodar along the road to Badrinath. That particular valley seems hostile to trees in general, and deodar in particular.

The average girth of the deodar varies from fifteen to twenty feet, but individual trees often attain a great size. Records show that one great deodar was 250 feet high, twenty feet in girth at the base, and more than 550 years old. The timber of these trees, which is unaffected by extremes of climate, was always highly prized for house-building, and in the villages of Jaunsar Bawar, finely carved doors and windows are a feature of the timbered dwellings. Many of the quaint old bridges over the Jhelum in Kashmir are supported on pillars fashioned from whole deodar trees; some of these bridges are more than 500 years old.

To return to my own trees, I went among them often, acknowledging their presence with a touch of my hand against their trunks—the walnut's smooth and polished; the pine's patterned and whorled; the oak's rough, gnarled, full of experience. The oak had been there the longest, and the wind had bent his upper branches and twisted a few, so that he looked shaggy and undistinguished. It is a good tree for the privacy of birds, its crooked branches spreading out with no particular effect; and sometimes the tree seems uninhabited until there is a whirring sound, as of a helicopter approaching, and a party of long-tailed blue magpies stream across the forest glade.

After the monsoon, when the dark red berries had ripened on the hawthorn, this pretty tree was visited by green pigeons, the kokla-birds of Garhwal, who clambered upside-down among the fruit-laden twigs. And during winter, a white-capped redstart perched on the bare branches of the wild pear tree and whistled cheerfully. He had come down from higher places to winter in the garden.

The pines grow on the next hill—the *chir*, the Himalayan blue pine, and the long-leaved pine—but there is a small blue pine a little way below the cottage, and sometimes I sit beneath it to listen to the wind playing softly in its branches.

Open the window at night, and there is usually something to listen to, the mellow whistle of the pygmy owlet, or the cry of a barking-deer which has scented the proximity of a panther.

Sometimes, if you are lucky, you will see the moon coming up, and two distant deodars in perfect silhouette.

Some sounds cannot be recognized. They are strange night sounds, the sounds of the trees themselves, stretching their limbs in the dark, shifting a little, flexing their fingers. Great trees of the mountains, they know me well. They know my face in the window; they see me watching them, watching them grow, listening to their secrets, bowing my head before their outstretched arms and seeking their benediction.

135

Walnut Tree Revisited

You have ripened, since last the walnut tree
Lost its dark leaves, last autumn.
One summer intervened between your growing
And my importunity;
One summer lost,
while walnuts grew;
I too had forgotten.

We saw each other often,
But gone was the magic
Of that first encounter;
And even the tree
Gave little fruit last year.
Now it stands bare-branched
Outside the closed window,
Touched no more by feet and questing fingers,
But turning its own fingers
To the slanting winter sun.
Not one leaf left, where hundreds
Glittered like spears in the forest of September.

But I will wait until the parrots bring
Shrill portents of another spring;
(And I will love you with the same sweet pain,
If you and summer care to visit me again.)

Picnic at Fox-Burn

IN SPITE OF the frenetic building activity in most hill-stations, there are still a few ruins to be found on the outskirts— neglected old bungalows that have fallen or been pulled down, and which now provide shelter for bats, owls, stray goats, itinerant sadhus, and sometimes the restless spirits of those who once dwelt in them.

One such ruin is Fox-Burn, but I won't tell you exactly where it can be found, because I visit the place for purposes of meditation (or just plain contemplation) and I would hate to arrive there one morning to find about fifty people picnicking on the grass.

And yet it did witness a picnic of sorts the other day, when the children accompanied me to the ruin. They had heard it was haunted, and they wanted to see the ghost.

Rakesh is twelve, Mukesh is six, and Dolly is four, and they are not afraid of ghosts.

I should mention here, that before Fox-Burn became a ruin, back in the 1940s, it was owned by an elderly English woman, Mrs Williams, who ran it as a boarding-house for several years. In the end, poor health forced her to give up this work, and during her last years, she lived alone in the huge house, with just a chowkidar to help. Her children, who had grown up on the property, had long since settled in faraway lands.

When Mrs Williams died, the chowkidar stayed on for some time until the property was disposed of; but he left as soon as he could. Late at night there would be a loud rapping on his door, and he would hear the old lady calling out: 'Shamsher Singh, open the door! Open the door, I say, and let me in!'

Needless to say, Shamsher Singh kept the door firmly closed. He returned to his village at the first opportunity. The hill-station was going through a slump at the time, and the new owners pulled the house down and sold the roof and beams as scrap.

'What does Fox-Burn mean?' asked Rakesh, as we climbed the neglected, overgrown path to the ruin.

'Well, Burn is a Scottish word meaning stream or spring. Perhaps there was a spring here, once. If so, it dried up long ago.'

'And did a fox live here?'

'Maybe a fox came to drink at the spring. There are still foxes living on the mountain. Sometimes you can see them dancing in the moonlight.'

Passing through a gap in a wall, we came upon the ruins of the house. In the bright light of a summer morning it did not look in the least spooky or depressing. A line of Doric pillars were all that remained of what must have been an elegant porch and veranda. Beyond them, through the deodars, we could see the distant snows. It must have been a lovely spot in which to spend the better part of one's life. No wonder Mrs Williams wanted to come back.

The children were soon scampering about on the grass, whilst I sought shelter beneath a huge chestnut tree.

There is no tree so friendly as the chestnut, especially in summer when it is in full leaf.

Mukesh discovered an empty water-tank and Rakesh suggested that it had once fed the burn that no longer existed. Dolly busied herself making nosegays with the daisies that grew wild in the grass.

Rakesh looked up suddenly. He pointed to a path on the other side of the ruin, and exclaimed: 'Look, what's that? Is it Mrs Williams?'

'A ghost!' said Mukesh excitedly.

But it turned out to be the local washerwoman, a large white bundle on her head, taking a short-cut across the property.

A more peaceful place could hardly be imagined, until a large black dog, a spaniel of sorts, arrived on the scene. He wanted someone to play with—indeed, he insisted on playing—and ran circles round us until we threw sticks for him to fetch and gave him half our sandwiches.

'Whose dog is it?' asked Rakesh.

'I've no idea.'

'Did Mrs Williams keep a black dog?'

'Is it a *ghost* dog?' asked Mukesh.

'It looks real to me,' I said.

'And it's eaten all my biscuits,' said Dolly.

'Don't ghosts have to eat?' asked Mukesh.

'I don't know. We'll have to ask one.'

'It can't be any fun being a ghost if you can't eat,' declared Mukesh.

The black dog left us as suddenly as he had appeared, and as there was no sign of an owner, I began to wonder if he had not, after all, been an apparition.

A cloud came over the sun, the air grew chilly.

'Let's go home,' said Mukesh.

'I'm hungry,' said Rakesh.

'Come along, Dolly,' I called.

But Dolly couldn't be seen.

We called out to her, and looked behind trees and pillars, certain that she was hiding from us. Almost five minutes passed in searching for her, and a sick feeling of apprehension was coming over me, when Dolly emerged from the ruins and ran towards us.

'Where have you been?' we demanded, almost with one voice.

'I was playing—in there—in the old house. Hide and seek.'

'On your own?'

'No, there were two children. A boy and a girl. They were playing too.'

'I haven't seen any children,' I said.

'They've gone now.'

'Well, it's time we went too.'

We set off down the winding path, with Rakesh leading the way, and then we had to wait because Dolly had stopped and was waving to someone.

'Who are you waving to, Dolly?'

'To the children.'

'Where are they?'

'Under the chestnut tree.'

'I can't see them. Can you see them, Rakesh? Can you, Mukesh?'

Rakesh and Mukesh said they couldn't see any children. But Dolly was still waving.

'Goodbye,' she called. 'Goodbye!'

Were there voices on the wind? Faint voices calling goodbye? Could Dolly see something we couldn't see?

'We can't see anyone,' I said.

'No,' said Dolly. 'But they can see me!'

Then she left off her game and joined us, and we ran home laughing. Mrs Williams may not have revisited her old house that day but perhaps her children had been there, playing under the chestnut tree they had known so long ago.

A Wayside Teashop

THE JAUNPUR RANGE in Garhwal is dry, brown and rocky. Water is hard to find, and green fields are to be seen only far down in the valley, near the Aglar or some smaller stream. Elsewhere only monsoon crops are grown.

I have walked five miles without finding a spring or even a shady spot along the sun-blistered path, and I am beginning to wonder if the only living creatures in the area are the big lizards, who slither about on the hot surface of the rocks and stare at me with unwinking eyes. Just as I am asking myself if it is better to be a lizard than a thirsty trekker, I round a bend and discover a small mountain oasis: a crooked little shack tucked away in a cleft of the hillside. Growing beside the shack is a single pine tree, humming softly in the faint breeze that drifts across the mountains.

When one tree suddenly appears in this way, lonely and dignified in the midst of a vast treeless silence, it can be more beautiful than a forest.

There is no glamour about the shack, a loose stone structure with a tin roof held down by stones. But it is a teashop, one of those little pockets of pioneering mankind that spring up in the mountain wilderness to serve the weary traveller. Go where you will in Garhwal, you will always find a teashop to sustain you just when you feel you have reached the end of your tether.

A couple of mules are tied to the pine tree, and the mule-drivers, handsome men in tattered clothes, sit on a bench in the shade, drinking tea from brass tumblers. The shopkeeper, a man of indeterminate age—the cold dry winds from the snows have crinkled his face like a walnut but his teeth are sound and his eyes are clear—greets me as a long-lost friend, although we are meeting for the first time.

As a concession to my shirt and trousers, he produces a chair for me. It is a period chair, possibly even a Sheraton, but the stuffing has come out of the seat. It must have escaped from the nearby hill-station of Mussoorie, where the sahibs foregathered in years gone by. The shopkeeper apologizes for its condition: 'The rats have been nesting in it.' And then, to reassure me, 'But they have gone now.'

I would just as soon be on the bench with the mule-drivers, but do not wish to offend the shopkeeper, who has already given me his name, Megh Chand, and taken mine. So I take his chair into the shade and gently lower myself into it.

'Do you live here alone?' I ask.

'Sometimes I am alone,' he says. 'My family is down in the village, looking after the fields. It is quite far, six miles. So I go home once a week, and then my son comes up to look after the shop.'

'How long have you had the shop?'

'Oh, ten–fifteen years, I do not remember exactly.'

Why bother to count the years? In remote mountain areas, time has a different meaning, you may count the days, but not the hours. And yesterday, today, and tomorrow merge into one long day. When there is nowhere to go, you have no need of a clock. You eat when you are hungry, and sleep when you are tired.

But the mule-drivers have somewhere to go and something to deliver: pumpkins and potatoes. They are busy men of the world, and presently they lead their pack-animals away down the dusty path.

'Tea or lassi?' Megh Chand gives me a choice, and I take the lassi, which is sharp and refreshing. The wind soughs gently in the upper branches of the pine tree and I relax in my Sheraton chair like some eighteenth century nabob who has brought his own chair into the wilderness.

Megh Chand tells me that he has been starved of good conversation. 'Next year,' he says, sitting down on the steps of his shop, 'the government will be widening the road, and then the buses will be able to stop here. For many years I have depended on the mule-drivers, but they do not have much money to spend. Once the buses come, I will have many customers. Then perhaps I can afford to go to Delhi to have my operation.'

'What operation?'

'Oh, a *rasoli*—a growth—in my stomach. Sometimes the pain is very bad. I went to the hospital in Mussoorie, but they told me I would have to go to Delhi for an operation. Whenever someone is seriously ill, they say, 'Go to Delhi!' Does the whole world go to Delhi to get treated? My uncle was told to go to Delhi for an operation. He went from one hospital to another until his money was finished, and then he came back to the village and died within a week. So maybe I won't go for the operation. The money is needed here. Once the buses come, I will have to keep sweets and biscuits and other things, and also a boy to help me cook a few meals. All I can offer you today is a bun. It was made in Delhi, I am told.'

'I'd rather have your lassi than a Delhi bun,' I protest, for the bun looks as old as the Sheraton chair. 'But where do you get your water?' I ask.

'Come, I will show you,' he says, and takes me round to the back of the shack and through an unexpected gap in the hillside. It gives me a breathtaking glimpse of snow-clad mountains striding into the sky. It is cool and shady on the northern face of the hill, and here, issuing from a rock, is a trickle of water. Yellow primulae grow in clusters along the edges of a damp, dripping rock-face. The water collects in a small stone trough.

'There is no other *cheshma* (spring) along this road,' he says, 'and the buses can't go down into the ravine, unless they fall into it. So they will have to stop here!' He is triumphant.

We return to the shop front, where a milkman has just arrived with a container of milk. He too sits down for rest, refreshment and conversation. Next year, if the road is ready (and it is a big if, because with hill roads you can never be sure), and if he can afford the fare (an even bigger if), the milkman will be able to use the bus. But there are some who will walk anyway, because they have always been walking. Or ride mules, because they have been doing it all their lives.

Still, when the road comes, time will take on new dimensions for Megh Chand. Even in remote mountain areas, buses must keep to some sort of schedule, and Megh Chand will have to be sure that his pot is on the boil, and be on the lookout for arrivals and departures. He will be better off than he is today but he is aware that prosperity has its pitfalls. He remembers a cousin, who opened a small grocery shop on a new bus-route near Devprayag. One day, some young hooligans got off the bus, looted his shop, and left him battered and bruised. It was the sort of thing that had never happened before . . . .

It is time for me to be on my way. I leave Megh Chand and his Sheraton chair with regret.

'I hope the road will soon be ready,' I say in parting. 'I hope you will make lots of money. I hope you will be able to go to Delhi for your operation. And I hope I can come this way again.'

Hillman or plainsman, we have only our hopes to keep us going.

❋

The Wind and the Rain

Like the wind, I run;
Like the rain, I sing;
Like the leaves, I dance;
Like the earth, I'm still;
And in this, Lord, I do thy will.

All About my Walkabouts

ALL MY LIFE I've been a walking person. Up to this day, I have neither owned nor driven a car, bus, tractor, airplane, motorcycle, truck, or steamroller. Forced to make a choice. I would as soon drive a steamroller, because of its slow but solid progress and unhurried finality. And also because other vehicles don't try hustling steamrollers off the road.

For a brief period in my early teens I had a bicycle, until I rode into a bullock cart and ruined my new cycle. The bullocks panicked and ran away with the cart while the furious cart driver was giving me a lecture on road sense. I have never bumped into a bullock cart while walking.

My earliest memories are of a place called Jamnagar, a small port on the west coast of India, then part of a princely state. My father was an English tutor to several young Indian princes and princesses. This was where my walking really began, because Jamnagar was full of spacious palaces, lawns, and gardens. By the time I was four, I was exploring much of this territory on my own, with the result that I encountered my first snake. Instead of striking me dead as snakes are supposed to do, it allowed me to pass.

Living as it did so close to the ground, and sensitive to every footfall, it must have known instinctively that I presented no threat, that I was just another small creature discovering the use of his legs. Envious of the snake's swift gliding movements, I went indoors and tried crawling about on my belly. But I wasn't much good at it. Legs were better.

My father's schoolroom and our own residence were located on the grounds of one of the older palaces, which was full of turrets, stairways, and mysterious dark passages. Right on top of the building I discovered a glass-covered room, each pane of glass stained with a different colour. This room fascinated me, as I could, by turn, look through the panes of glass at a green or rose-pink or orange or deep indigo world. It was nice to be able to decide for oneself what colour the world should be!

My father took his duties seriously and taught me to read and write long before I started attending a regular school. However, it would be true to say that I first learned to read upside down. This happened because I would sit on a stool in front of the three princesses, watching them read and write, and so the view I had of their books was an upside-down view, I still read that way occasionally, especially when a book becomes boring.

There was no boredom in the palace grounds. We were situated in the middle of a veritable jungle of a garden, where marigolds and cosmos grew, rampant in the long grass. An old disused well was the home of countless pigeons, their gentle cooing by day contrasting with the shrill cries of the brain-fever bird (the hawk-cuckoo) at night. 'How very hot it's getting!' the bird seems to say. And then, in a rising crescendo, 'We feel it! *We feel it!* WE FEEL IT!'

Walking along a nearby beach, collecting seashells, I got into the habit of staring hard at the ground, a habit which has remained with me all my life. Apart from helping my thought processes, it also results in my picking up odd objects—coins, keys, broken bangles, marbles, pens, bits of crockery, pretty stones, feathers, ladybirds, seashells, snail-shells! Not to speak of old nails and horseshoes. Looking at my collection of miscellaneous objects picked up on these walks, my friends insist that I must be using a metal detector. But it's only because I keep my nose to the ground, like a bloodhound.

Occasionally, of course, this habit results in my walking some way past my destination (if I happen to have one). And why not? It simply means discovering a new and different destination, sights and sounds that I might not have experienced had I ended my walk exactly where it was supposed to end. And I am not looking at the ground *all* the time. Sensitive like the snake to approaching footfalls, I look up from time to time to take note of the faces of passers-by, just in case they have something interesting to say.

A bird singing in a bush or tree has my immediate attention, so does any familiar flower or plant, particularly if it grows in an unusual place such as a crack in a wall or rooftop, or in a yard full of junk—where once I found a rosebush blooming on the roof of an old, abandoned Ford car.

I like to think that I invented the zigzag walk. Tiring of walking in straight lines, or on roads that led directly to a destination, I took to going off at tangents—taking sudden unfamiliar turnings, wandering down narrow alleyways, following cart tracks or paths through fields instead of the main roads, and in general making the walk as complicated as possible.

In this way I saw much more than I would normally have seen. Here a temple, there a mosque; now an old church; a railway siding; follow the railway line; here's a pond full of buffaloes, there a peacock preening itself under a tamarind tree; and now I'm in a field of mustard, and soon I'm walking along a canal bank, and the canal leads me back into the town, and I follow the line of the mango trees until I am home.

The adventure is not in arriving, it's the on-the-way experience. It is not the expected; it's the surprise. You are not choosing what you shall see in the world, but are giving the world an even chance to see you.

It's like drawing lines from star to star in the night sky, not forgetting many dim, shy, out-of-the-way stars, which are full of possibilities. The first turning to the left, the next to the right! I am still on my zigzag way, pursuing the diagonal between reason and the heart.

Great Spirits of the Trees

EXPLORE THE HISTORY and mythology of almost any Indian tree, and you will find that at some period of our civilization it has held an important place in the minds and hearts of the people of this land.

During the rains, when the neem-pods fall and are crushed underfoot, they give out a strong refreshing aroma which lingers in the air for days. This is because the neem gives out more oxygen than most trees. When the ancient herbalists held that the neem was a great purifier of the air, and that its leaves, bark and sap had medicinal qualities, they were quite right, for the neem is still used in medicine today.

From the earliest times it was connected with the gods who protect us from disease. Some castes regarded the tree as sacred to Sitala, the smallpox goddess. When children fell ill, a branch of the neem was waved over them. The tree is said to have sprung from the nectar of the gods, and people still chew the leaves as a means of purification, both spiritual and physical.

The tree is also connected with the sun, as in the story of neem-barak, 'The Sun in the Neem Tree'. The Sun God invited to dinner a man of the Bairagi tribe whose rules forbade him to eat except by daylight. Dinner was late, and as darkness fell, the Bairagi feared he would have to go hungry. But Suraj Narayan, the Sun God, descended from a neem tree and continued shining till dinner was over.

Why have so many trees been held sacred, not only in India but the world over?

To early man they were objects of awe and wonder. The mystery of their growth, the movement of their leaves and branches, the way they seemed to die and then come to life again in spring, the sudden growth of the plant from the seed, all these happenings appeared as miracles—as indeed they are! And because of the wonderful growth of a tree, people began to suppose that it was occupied by spirits, and devotion to a tree became devotion to the spirit or tree-god who occupied it.

In *Puck of Pook's Hill*, Kipling wove some wonderful stories, around Puck, the tree-spirit, and the sacred trees of Old England—oak, ash and thorn: 'I came into England with Oak, Ash, and Thorn, and when Oak, Ash and Thorn are gone, I shall go too.'

Among the Gonds of Central India, before a man cut a tree he had to beg its pardon for the injury he was about to inflict on it. He would not shake a tree at night because the tree-spirit was asleep and might be disturbed. When a tree had to be felled, the Gonds would pour ghee on the stump, saying: 'Grow thou out of this, O Lord of the Forest, grow into a hundred shoots! May we grow with a thousand shoots.'

The beautiful mahua is a forest tree held sacred by a number of tribes. Early on the wedding morning, before he goes to fetch his bride, the Bagdi bridegroom goes through a mock marriage with a mahua tree. He embraces it and daubs it with vermilion, his right wrist is bound to it with thread, and after he is released from the tree the thread is used to attach a bunch of mahua leaves to his wrist.

There is a beautiful tradition connected with the sal tree. It is said that at the time of the Buddha's birth, his mother stretched out her hand to take hold of a branch of the sal and was delivered. Sal trees are also said to have rendered homage to the Buddha at his death, letting fall on him their flowers out of season, and bending their branches to shade him.

Special respect is paid to trees growing near the graves of Muslim saints. Near the tomb of a famous saint, Musa Sohag, at Ahmedabad, there used to be a large old champa tree—perhaps it is still there—the branches of which were hung with glass bangles. Those anxious to have children came and offered bangles to the saint—the number of bangles depending on the means of the supplicant. If the saint favoured a wish, the champa tree snatched up the bangles and wore them on its arms'.

Another spectacular tree which has its place in our folklore

149

is the dhak, or palasa, which gave its name to the battlefield of Plassey. It has the habit of dropping its leaves when it flowers, the upper and outer branches standing out in sprays of scarlet and orange. The flowers are sometimes used to dye the powder scattered at Holi, the spring festival; and the wood, said to contain the seed of fire, is used in lighting the Holi bonfire. Legend tells us that the Sun God aimed an arrow at the earth, and that it took root and became the palasa tree.

The babul (or keekar) is not very impressive to look at but it will grow almost anywhere in the plains, and there are a number of old beliefs associated with it. For instance, you can cure fever and headache at a babul tree if you tie seven cotton threads from your left big toe to your head, and from your head to a branch of the tree. Then you must embrace the trunk seven times. Try it sometime. You will be so busy tying threads that you will forget you ever had a headache! And there are no after-effects.

Another belief concerning the babul is that if you water it regularly for thirteen days, you acquire control over the spirit who occupies it. There is a story about a man at Saharanpur who did this, and when he died and his corpse was taken away for cremation, no sooner was his pyre lit than he got up and walked away!

In the folklore of India, the mango is the 'wish-fulfilling tree'. When you want to make a wish on a mango tree, shut your eyes and get someone to lead you to the tree; then rub mango blossoms in your hands, and make your wish. The favour granted lasts only for a year, and the charm must be performed again at the next flowering of the tree. In the spring, the young leaves and buds symbolize the darts of Manmatha, or Kamadeva, God of Love.

Another 'wishing tree', the kalp-vriksha, is an enormous old mulberry that is still cared for at Joshimath in Garhwal. It is said to be the tree beneath which the great Sankaracharya often meditated during his sojourn in the Himalayas. Judging by its girth, it might well be over a thousand years old.

Whole forests have been held sacred, such as that in Berar which was dedicated to a particular temple; no one dared to buy or cut the trees. The sacred groves near Mathura, where Lord Krishna sported as a youth, were also protected for centuries. But now, alas, even the hallowed groves are disappearing, making way for the demands of an ever-increasing population. A pity, because every human needs a tree of his own. Even if you do not worship the tree-spirit, you can love the tree.

So Beautiful the Night

I love the night, Lord.
After the sun's heat and the day's work,
it's good to close my eyes and rest my body.
It's a good time for small creatures:
Porcupines come out of their burrows
to dig for roots.
The night-jar calls tonk-tonk!
The timid owl peeps out of his hole in the tree trunk
Where he has been hiding all day.
Insects crawl out in thousands.
The wind comes down the chimney
and blows around the room.
I'm watching the stars from my window.
The trees are stretching their arms in the dark
and whispering to the moon.
But if the trees could walk, Lord,
What a wonderful sight it would be—
Armies of pines and firs and oaks
Marching over the moonlit mountains.

Birdsong Heard in the Mountains

BIRD-WATCHING IS more difficult in the hills than on the plains. It is hard to spot many birds against the dark trees of the varying shades of the hillside.

There are few birds who remain silent for long, however, and one learns of their presence from their calls or songs. Birdsong is with you wherever you go in the Himalayas, from the foothills to the tree-line; and it is often easier to recognize a bird from its voice than from its colourful but brief appearance.

The barbet is one of those birds which is heard more often than it is seen. It has a monotonous, far-reaching call, which carries for about a mile. These birds love listening to their own voices, and often two or three will answer each other from different trees, each trying to outdo the rest in a shrill shouting match. Some people like the barbet's call and consider it both striking and pleasant. Some just find it striking.

Hodgson's grey-headed flycatcher-warbler is the long name that ornithologists, in their infinite wisdom, have given to a very small bird. This tiny warbler is heard, if not seen, more often than any other bird throughout the western Himalayas. Its voice is heard in every second tree, and yet there are few who can say what it looks like. Its song (if you can call it that), is not very tuneful and puts me in mind of the notice that sometimes appeared in saloons out West: 'The audience is requested not to throw things at the pianist. He is doing his best.'

Our little warbler does his best, incessantly emitting four or five unmusical, but nevertheless joyful and penetrating notes.

Another tiny bird heard more often than it is seen is the green-backed tit, a smart little fellow about the size of a sparrow. It utters a sharp, rather metallic, but not unpleasant call which sounds like '*kiss me, kiss me, kiss me*'.

A real songster is the grey-winged ouzel, found here in the Garhwal hills. Throughout the early summer he makes the wooded hillsides ring with a melody that Nelson Eddy would have been proud of. Joining in sometimes with a sweet song of its own, is the green pigeon. As though to mock their arias, the laughing-thrushes, who are exponents of heavy rock, give vent to some weird calls of their own.

Nightjars are birds that lie concealed during the day in shady woods, coming out at dusk on silent wings to hunt for insects. The nightjar has a huge, froglike mouth, but is best recognized by its unusual call—'*tonk-tonk, tonk-tonk*'— a noise like that produced by striking a plank with a hammer.

When I first came to live in the hills, it was the song of the Himalayan whistling-thrush that first caught my attention. I was sitting at my window, gazing out at the new leaves on the walnut tree. All was still; the wind was at peace with itself, the mountains brooded massively under a darkening sky. Then, emerging like a sweet secret from the depths of a deep ravine, came this indescribably beautiful call.

It is a song that never fails to enchant me. The bird starts with a hesitant whistle, as though trying out the tune; then, confident of the melody, it bursts into full song, a crescendo of sweet notes and variations ringing clearly across the hillside. Suddenly the song breaks off, right in the middle of a cadenza, and I am left wondering what happened to make the bird stop. Nothing really, because the song is taken up again a few moments later.

One day I saw the whistling-thrush perched on the broken garden fence. He was a deep, glistening purple, his shoulders flecked with white. He had sturdy black legs and a strong yellow beak; a dapper fellow who would have looked just right in a top hat. As time passed, he 'grew accustomed to my face' and became a regular visitor to the garden. On sultry summer afternoons I would find him flapping about in the water-tank. Later, refreshed and sunning himself on the roof, he would treat me to a little concert before flying off to his shady ravine.

It was a boy from the next village who acquainted me with

the legend of the whistling-thrush.

According to the story, the young god, Krishna fell asleep near a stream, and while he slept a small boy made off with Krishna's famous flute. Upon waking and finding his flute gone, Krishna was so angry that he changed the culprit into a bird. But having once played on the flute, the boy had learnt bits and pieces of the god's enchanting music. And so he continued, in his disrespectful way, to play the music of the gods, only stopping now and then (as the whistling-thrush does), when he couldn't remember the tune.

It wasn't long before my whistling-thrush was joined by a female. Were they Jeanette MacDonald and Nelson Eddy reincarnated? Sometimes they gave solo performances, sometimes they sang duets; and these latter, no doubt, were love-calls, because it wasn't long before the pair were making forays into the rocky ledges of the ravine. looking for a suitable nesting site.

The birds were liveliest in midsummer; but even in the depths of winter, with snow lying on the ground, they would suddenly start singing, as they flitted from pine to oak to naked chestnut.

The wild cherry tree, which grows just outside my bedroom window, attracts a great many small birds, both when it is in flower and when it is in fruit.

When it is covered with small pink blossoms, the most common visitor is a little yellow-backed sunbird, who emits a squeaky little song as she flits from branch to branch. She extracts the nectar from the blossoms with her long tubular tongue.

Amongst other visitors are the flycatchers, gorgeous birds, especially the paradise flycatcher with its long white tail and ghost-like flight. Basically an insect-eater, it likes fruit for dessert, and will visit the tree when the cherries are ripening. While moving along the boughs of the tree, they utter twittering notes, with occasional louder calls, and now and then the male breaks into a sweet little song, thus justifying the name of *shah bulbul* (king of the nightingales), by which he is known in northern India.

Boy in a Blue Pullover

Boy in a faded blue pullover,
Poor boy, thin, smiling boy,
Ran down the road shouting,
Singing, flinging his arms wide.
I stood in the way and stopped him.
'What's up?' I said. 'Why are you happy?'
He showed me the nickel rupee-coin.
'I found it on the road,' he said.
And he held it to the light
That he might see it shining bright.
'And how will you spend it,
Small boy in blue pullover?'
'I'll buy—
I'll buy a buckle for my belt !
Slim boy, smart boy,
Would buy a buckle for his belt
Coin clutched in his hot hand,
He ran off laughing, bright.
The coin I'd lost an hour ago;
But better his that night.

Meetings on the Tehri Road

THE HUMAN PERSONALITY can impose its own nature on its surroundings. At a dark, windy corner in the bazaar, one always found an old man hunched up over his charcoal fire, roasting peanuts. He died last summer.

Then, a few weeks ago, there was a new occupant of the corner, a new seller of peanuts. No relative of the old man; but a boy of thirteen or fourteen, cheerful, involved, exchanging good-natured banter with his customers. In the old man's time it seemed a dark, gloomy corner. Now it's lit up by sunshine; a sunny personality, smiling, chattering. Old age gives way to youth; and I'm glad I won't be alive when the new peanut-vendor grows old. One shouldn't see too many people grow old.

Leaving the main bazaar behind, I walk some way down the Mussoorie–Tehri road, a fine road to walk on, in spite of the dust from an occasional bus or jeep. From Mussoorie to Chamba, a distance of some thirty-five miles, the road seldom descends below 7,000 feet, and there is a continual vista of the snow ranges to the north and the valleys and rivers to the south. Dhanolti is one of the lovelier spots, and the Garhwal Mandal has a rest-house here, where one can spend an idyllic weekend. Some years ago I walked all the way to Chamba, spending the night at Kaddu-khal, from where a short climb takes one to the Sirkhanda Devi temple.

Leaving the Tehri road, one can also trek down to the little Aglar river and then up to Nag Tibba, 9,000 feet, which has a good oak forest and animals ranging from barking-deer to Himalayan bear; but this is an arduous trek and you must be prepared to spend the night in the open or seek the hospitality of a village.

Having wandered some way down the Tehri road, it is quite late by the time I return to the Landour bazaar. Lights still twinkle on the hills, but shop fronts are shuttered and the little bazaar is silent. The people living on either side of the narrow street can hear my footsteps, and I can hear their casual remarks, music, a burst of laughter.

Through a gap in the rows of buildings I can see Pari Tibba outlined in the moonlight. A greenish phosphorescent glow appears to move here and there about the hillside. This is the 'fairy light' that gives the hill its name—Pari Tibba, Fairy Hill. I have no explanation for it, and I don't know anyone else who has been able to explain it satisfactorily; but often from my window I see this greenish light zigzagging about the hill.

A three-quarter moon is up, and the tin roofs of the bazaar, drenched with dew, glisten in the moonlight. Although the street is unlit, I need no torch. I can see every step of the way. I can even read the headlines on the discarded newspaper lying in the gutter.

Although I am alone on the road, I am aware of the life pulsating around me. It is a cold night, doors and windows are shut; but through the many chinks, narrow fingers of light reach out into the night. Who could still be up? A shopkeeper going through his accounts, a college student preparing for his exams, someone coughing and groaning in the dark.

Three stray dogs are romping in the middle of the road. It is their road now, and they abandon themselves to a wild chase, almost knocking me down.

The rickshaw stand is deserted. One rickshaw catches the eye because it is decorated with dahlias and marigolds, most of them still fresh.

A jackal slinks across the road, looking right then left—he knows his road-drill—to make sure the dogs have gone. A field rat wriggles through a hole in a rotting plank on its nightly foray among sacks of grain and pulses.

Yes, this is an old bazaar. The bakers, tailors, silversmiths and wholesale merchants are the grandsons of those who followed the mad sahibs to this hill-top in the Thirties and Forties of the last century. Most of them are plainsmen, quite prosperous even though many of their houses are crooked and shaky.

Although the shopkeepers and tradesmen are fairly prosperous, the hill people—those who come from the surrounding Tehri and Jaunpur villages—are usually poor. Their small holdings and rocky fields do not provide them with much of a living, and men and boys have often to come into the hill-station or go down to the cities in search of a livelihood. They pull rickshaws, or work in hotels and restaurants. Most of them have somewhere to stay.

But as I pass along the deserted street, under the shadow of the clock tower, I find a boy huddled in a recess, a thin shawl wrapped around his shoulders. He is wide awake and shivering.

I pass by, head down, my thoughts already on the warmth of my small cottage only a mile away. And then I stop. It is almost as though the bright moonlight has stopped me, holding my shadow in thrall.

> *If I am not for myself,*
> *Who will be for me?*
> *And if I am not for others,*
> *What am I*
> *And if not now, when?*

The words of an ancient sage beat upon my mind. I walk back to the shadows where the boy crouches. He does not say anything, but he looks up at me, puzzled and apprehensive. All the warnings of well-wishers crowd in upon me—stories of crime by night, of assault and robbery, 'ill met by moonlight . . . .'

But this is not Northern Ireland or the Lebanon or the streets of New York. This is Landour in the Garhwal Himalayas. And the boy is no criminal. I can tell from his features that he comes from the hills beyond Tehri. He has come here looking for work and he has yet to find any.

'Have you somewhere to stay?' I ask. He shakes his head; but something about my tone of voice has given him confidence, because now there is a glimmer of hope, a friendly appeal in his eyes.

I have committed myself. I cannot pass on. A shelter for the night—that's the very least one human should be able to expect from another.

'If you can walk some way,' I offer, 'I can give you a bed and blanket.'

He gets up immediately—a thin boy, wearing only a shirt and part of an old track-suit. He follows me without any hesitation. I cannot now betray his trust. Nor can I fail to trust him.

So now there are two in the sleeping moonlit bazaar. I glance up at the tall, packed houses. They seem to lean towards each other for warmth and companionship.

The boy walks silently besides me. Soon we are out of the bazaar and on the footpath. The mountains loom over us. A fox dances in the moonlight and a night-bird calls. And although no creature of the forest has ever harmed me, I am glad to have a companion as I walk towards another Himalayan dawn.

The Bat

Most bats fly high,
Swooping only
To take some insect on the wing;
But there's a bat I know
Who flies so low
He skims the floor;
He does not enter at the window
But flies in at the door,
Does stunts beneath the furniture.

Is his radar wrong,
Or does he just prefer
Being different from other bats?
I've grown quite used to him:
He appeals to the paradox in me.
And when sometimes
He settles upside down
At the foot of my bed,
I let him be.
On lonely nights, even a crazy bat
Is company.

Guests who Fly in from the Forest

W HEN MIST FILLS the Himalayan valleys, and heavy monsoon rain sweeps across the hills, it is natural for wild creatures to seek shelter. Any shelter is welcome in a storm—and sometimes my cottage in the forest is the most convenient refuge.

There is no doubt that I make things easier for all concerned by leaving most of my windows open—I am one of those peculiar people who like to have plenty of fresh air indoors—and if a few birds, beasts and insects come in too, they're welcome, provided they don't make too much of a nuisance of themselves.

I must confess that I did lose patience with a bamboo beetle who blundered in the other night and fell into the water jug. I rescued him and pushed him out of the window. A few seconds later he came whirring in again, and with unerring accuracy landed with a plop in the same jug. I fished him out once more and offered him the freedom of the night. But attracted no doubt by the light and warmth of my small sitting-room, he came buzzing back, circling the room like a helicopter looking for a good place to land. Quickly I covered the water jug. He landed in a bowl of wild dahlias, and I allowed him to remain there, comfortably curled up in the hollow of a flower.

Sometimes, during the day, a bird visits me—a deep purple whistling-thrush, hopping about on long dainty legs, peering to right and left, too nervous to sing. She perches on the windowsill, looking out at the rain. She does not permit any familiarity. But if I sit quietly in my chair, she will sit quietly on her windowsill, glancing quickly at me now and then just to make sure that I'm keeping my distance. When the rain stops, she glides away, and it is only then, confident in her freedom, that she bursts into full-throated song, her broken but haunting melody echoing down the ravine.

A squirrel comes sometimes, when his home in the oak tree gets waterlogged. Apparently he is a bachelor; anyway, he lives alone. He knows me well, this squirrel, and is bold enough to climb on to the dining-table looking for tidbits which he always finds, because I leave them there deliberately. Had I met him when he was a youngster, he would have learned to eat from my hand; but I have only been here a few months. I like it this way. I am not looking for pets: these are simply guests.

Last week, as I was sitting down at my desk to write a long-deferred article, I was startled to see an emerald-green praying mantis sitting on my writing pad. He peered up at me with his protruberant glass bead eyes, and I stared down at him through my reading glasses. When I gave him a prod, he moved off in a leisurely way. Later I found him examining the binding of Whitman's *Leaves of Grass*; perhaps he had found a succulent bookworm. He disappeared for a couple of days, and then I found him on the dressing-table, preening himself before the mirror. Perhaps I am doing him an injustice in assuming that he was preening. Maybe he thought he'd met another mantis and was simply trying to make contact. Anyway, he seemed fascinated by his reflection.

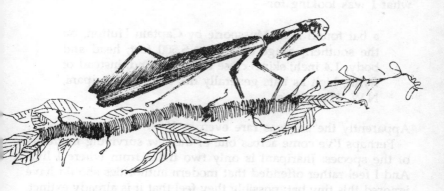

Out in the garden, I spotted another mantis, perched on the jasmine bush. Its arms were raised like a boxer's. Perhaps they're a pair, I thought, and went indoors and fetched my mantis and placed him on the jasmine bush, opposite his fellow insect. He did not like what he saw—no comparison with his own image!—and made off in a huff.

My most interesting visitor comes at night, when the lights are still burning—a tiny bat who prefers to fly in at the door, should it be open, and will use the window only if there's no alternative. His object in entering the house is to snap up the moths that cluster around the lamps.

All the bats I've seen fly fairly high, keeping near the ceiling as far as possible, and only descending to ear level (my ear level) when they must; but this particular bat flies in low, like a dive bomber, and does acrobatics amongst the furniture, zooming in and out of chair legs and under tables. Once, while careening about the room in this fashion, he passed straight between my legs.

Has his radar gone wrong, I wondered, or is he just plain crazy?

I went to my shelves of *Natural History* and looked up Bats, but could find no explanation for this erratic behaviour. As a last resort, I turned to an ancient volume, Sterndale's *Indian Mammalia* (Calcutta, 1884), and in it, to my delight, I found what I was looking for—

> a bat found near Mussoorie by Captain Hutton, on the southern range of hills at 5,500 feet; head and body, 1.4 inch; skims close to the ground, instead of flying high as bats generally do, Habitat, Jharipani, N.W. Himalayas.

Apparently the bat was rare even in 1884.

Perhaps I've come across one of the few surviving members of the species: Jharipani is only two miles from where I live. And I feel rather offended that modern authorities should have ignored this tiny bat; possibly they feel that it is already extinct. If so, I'm pleased to have rediscovered it. I am happy that it survives in my small corner of the woods, and I undertake to celebrate it in prose and verse.

A Bedbug Gives Thanks

I'm a child of the Universe
Claimed the bug
As he crawled out of the woodwork.
I've every right
To be a blight.
To Infinite Intelligence I owe
My place—
Chief pest
Upon the human race!
I'm here to stay—
To feast upon their delicate display,
Those luscious thighs,
Those nooks and crannies
Where the blood runs sweet.
No, no, I don't despise
These creatures made for my delight.
A kind Creator had my needs in mind . . . . .
I thank you, Lord, for human-kind.

Up at Sisters Bazaar

A FEW YEARS ago I spent a couple of summers up at Sisters Bazaar, at the farthest extremity of Mussoorie's Landour cantonment—an area as yet untouched by the tentacles of a bulging, disoriented octopus of a hill-station.

There were a number of residences up at Sisters, most of them old houses, but they were at some distance from each other, separated by clumps of oak or stands of deodar. After sundown, flying-foxes swooped across the roads, and the nightjar set up its nocturnal chant. Here, I thought, I would live like Thoreau at Walden Pond—alone, aloof, far from the strife and cacophony of the vast amusement park that was now Mussoorie. How wrong I was proved to be!

To begin with, I found that almost everyone on the hillside was busily engaged in writing a book. Was the atmosphere really so conducive to creative activity, or was it just a conspiracy to put me out of business? The discovery certainly put me out of my stride completely, and it was several weeks before I could write a word.

There was a retired Brigadier who was writing a novel about World War II, and a retired Vice-Admiral who was writing a book about a Rear Admiral. Mrs S, who had been an actress in the early days of the talkies, was writing poems in the manner of Wordsworth; and an ageing (or rather, resurrected) ex-Maharani was penning her memoirs. There was also an elderly American who wrote salacious best-selling novels about India. It was said of him that he looked like Hemingway and wrote like Charles Bronson.

With all this frenzied literary activity going on around me, it wasn't surprising that I went into shock for some time.

I was saved (or so I thought) by a 'far-out' ex-hippie and

ex-Hollywood scriptwriter who decided he would produce a children's film based on one of my stories. It was a pleasant little story, and all would have gone well if our producer friend hadn't returned from some high-altitude poppy fields in a bit of a trance and failed to notice that his leading lady was in the family way. Although the events of the story all took place in a single day, the film itself took about four months to complete, with the result that her figure altered considerably from scene to scene until, by late evening of the same day, she was displaying all the glories of imminent motherhood.

Naturally, the film was never released. I believe our producer friend now runs a health-food restaurant in Sydney.

I shared a large building (it had paper-thin walls), with several other tenants, one of whom, a French girl in her thirties, was learning to play the sitar. She and her tabla-playing companion would sleep by day, but practise all through the night, making sleep impossible for me or anyone else in my household. I would try singing operatic arias to drown her out, but you can't sing all night and she always outlasted me. Even a raging forest fire, which forced everyone else to evacuate the building for a night, did not keep her from her sitar any more than Rome burning kept Nero from his fiddle. Finally I got one of the chowkidar's children to pour sand into her instrument, and that silenced her for some time.

Another tenant who was there for a short while was a Dutchman, (yes, we were a cosmopolitan lot in the 1980s, before visa regulations were tightened) who claimed to be an acupuncturist. He showed me his box of needles and promised to cure me of the headaches that bothered me from time to time. But before he could start the treatment, he took a tumble while coming home from a late night party and fell down the khud into a clump of cacti, the sharp-pointed kind, which punctured the more tender parts of his anatomy. He had to spend a couple of weeks in the local mission hospital, receiving more conventional treatment, and he never did return to cure my headaches.

How did Sisters Bazaar come by its name?

Well, in the bad old, good old days, when Landour was a

convalescent station for sick and weary British soldiers, the nursing sisters had their barracks in the long, low building that lines the road opposite Prakash's Store. On the old maps this building is called 'The Sisters'. For a time it belonged to Dev Anand's family, but I believe it has since changed hands.

Of a 'bazaar' there is little evidence, although Prakash's Store must be at least a hundred years old. It is famous for its home-made cheese, and tradition has it that several generations of the Nehru family have patronized the store, from Motilal Nehru in the 1920s, to Rahul and his mother in more recent times.

I am more of a jam-fancier myself, and although I no longer live in the area, I do sometimes drop into the store for a can of raspberry or apricot or plum jam, made from the fruit brought here from the surrounding villages.

Further down the road is Dahlia Bank, where dahlias once covered the precipitous slope (known as the 'Eyebrow'), behind the house. The old military hospital, (which was opened in 1827) has been altered and expanded to house the present Defence Institute of Work Study. Beyond it lies Mount Hermon, with the lonely grave of a lady who perished here one wild and windy winter, 150 years ago. And close by lies the lovely Oakville Estate, where at least three generations of the multi-talented Alter family have lived. They do everything from acting in Hindi films to climbing greasy poles, Malkhumb-style. From wise old Bob to Steve and Andy, those Alter boys are mighty handy.

It is cold up there in winter, and I now live about 500 feet lower down, where it is only slightly warmer. But my walks take me up the hill from time to time. Most of the unusual eccentric people I have written about have gone away, but others, equally interesting, have taken their place. But for news of them you'll have to wait for my autobiography. The Mussoorie gossips will then get a dose of their own medicine. Let them start having sleepless nights.

NOTES
BY THE
WAYSIDE

*From a
Writer's
Logbook*

1982

22 February

After a month's absence, Prem and the family back from the village. Mukesh's head in bandage, having tumbled down the steps of the village house; but he is mending fast. He was two last month.

14 March

After being out of print for twenty years, *The Room on the Roof* is reprinted in an edition for schools, largely due to my own efforts and the foresight of the Students' Stores. Mr Sharma, the publisher, tells me the convent nuns don't approve of Rusty kissing Meena in the forest, but he hopes to override their objections.

21 March

Bad weather over Holi. Room flooded. Everyone down with septic throats and fever. While abed, read Stendhal's *Scarlet and Black*. Most of my serious reading seems to get done when I'm sick. No better way of recuperating!

28 March

Felt well enough to take a leisurely walk along the Tehri road. Trees in new leaf. The fresh young green of the maples particularly soothing. I thought: I may not have contributed anything to the progress of mankind, but neither have I robbed the world of anything—not one tree or bird or wildflower. Well, maybe the odd flower. Can't resist plucking dandelions.

6 April

Raki's turn to fall on his head. Five stitches and a black eye. He'll be eight this year.

11 April

Swifts busy nesting in the roof and performing aerobatics outside my window. They do everything on the wing, it seems—including feeding and making love. Making love in mid-air is probably more fun than doing it while static. They cannot perch in the normal way.

The spring's first ladybird on my windowsill.

6 May

A local racketeer, who has been in jail a couple of times, complimented me because I was 'always smiling'. I thought better of him for the observation. Flattery will get you everywhere!

'We are all worms,' declared Winston Churchill in 1906. 'But I do believe that I am a glow-worm.'

1 July

New regime. Stay slim with sex.

1 August

It didn't work.

10 July

Seventh impression of *Grandfather's Private Zoo*—these stories are my inheritance from Grandfather. Could he really have kept so many birds and animals in the house?

18 July

First clear morning after days of rain. Usha brings flowers—hydrangea, gladioli, dahlias. A lovely girl, the roses blooming in her cheeks.

5 *August*

Managed an article a day for over a month. Grub Street again!

'Never despair. But if you do, then work in despair.' (I don't know who said that, but I remember reading the lines while I was at school.)

6 *August*

Dare

Will

Keep Silence

And thank God for *The Tribune* of Chandigarh.

25 *August*

Shortage of cash. Muddle, muddle, toil and trouble. Learn to zigzag!

'We shall not spoil what we have by desiring what we have not, but remember that what we have too was the gift of fortune.'

(**Epicurus**)

15 *September*

'We ought to have more sense, of course, than to try to touch a dream or to reach that place which exists but in the glamour of a name.

(**H. M. Tomlinson**, *Tide Marks*, 1924)

'Kota Bharu . . . . It has a rest-house, a rambling and capacious building of timber, where I thought it would be easy to stay for so long that one might forget to go.'

(*Tide Marks*)

This is what happened to me in Mussoorie. I forgot to go. First it was Maplewood Lodge. And now Ivy Cottage . . . .

23 *September*

Zoo royalties and *Monitor* cheque to the rescue. We live to fight another day!

27 October

Savitri (Dolly) is one. She'll grow into a bonny girl.

And it's been a good year for the cosmos flower. Banks of them everywhere. They like the day-long sun. Clean and fresh—my favourite flower *en masse*.

By itself, the wild commelina, reflecting the blue of the sky, always catches at my heart.

28 October

If you have one true friend, you have more than your share.

31 October

Be proud. Be proud of what you are and what you've done. But be proud *within*. Don't flaunt it, you will only offend. There's something obscene about a braggart.

17 November

A boy stretches out on the bench like a cat, and the setting sun is trapped in his eyes, golden brown, glowing like a tiger's eyes. He reminds me a little of Somi as a boy. (Somi of *The Room on the Roof*.) Not only physically, but the same lilting laughter.

4 December

Someone came up to me in the dark (on the road outside the cottage) and kissed me and ran away. Who could it have been? So soft and warm and all-encompassing . . . . The moment stayed with me all night . . . .

Light snowfall by morning. Just enough to cloak the deodars for an hour or two, before it all melted away.

1983

5 January

Raki writes from the village: little ones and their mother unhappy. Send Prem to fetch them.

10 January

Prem returns with the family.

'You know, the way love can change a fellow is really frightful to contemplate.'

(P. G. Wodehouse)

11 March

Feeling a bit low, so I played marbles with the children, and they won all my marbles. Felt better. Rode Raki's rickety cycle. Fell off. Felt better.

30 April

So finally I have moved to the top of the mountain. It's colder up here, a thousand feet higher than the town, and the town is six thousand feet above sea-level. The 'foliage is superior', as a young trainee-diplomat remarked to me the other day. He meant they there were more trees.

There are three or four shops in the bazaar—a general store, a bania's ration-shop, a boutique for the tourists, and a small tea-shop for the locals.

It's a cantonment area, neat, clean, well-maintained. Therefore the trees. In a civil area, the contractors would have had them long ago.

But it's a small cantonment. Only a few officers and their families. A small staff. No soldiers on parade.

On the southern slopes, missionaries, mostly American.

On the northern face, some foreign residents, occasional scholars (a bit vague about what they are studying or researching), trippers, 'hippies' (the term still lingers here) doing their thing, which is mostly smoking *charas*.

Up from the villages the milkmen come. And from the town, the bakers and other tradesmen.

A few wealthy Indians have their houses here. They come in the summer, like migrant birds. Stay a week or two, then vanish in their limousines.

*

Mornings, I walk Raki down to school. All the way down the hill and through the Landour bazaar (just coming to life) and up the road past the clock tower to St. Clare's. I have to tell him stories on the way. As I was running out of ideas, I made up this man-eating leopard who terrorizes the hillside, snapping up a human victim every day. As long as there are suitable victims, I can keep the serial going. 'But when   asks Raki, 'is someone going to kill it?'

'You don't want the story to end, do you?' I ask. 'We have a population of ten thousand in this town. Let's see how many survive.

'If there were two leopards, it would be quicker   says Raki.

I walk up alone, huffing and puffing all the way, it's one long steep climb, and the road doesn't level out until you're at the church. On the way I pass other children going to school (most of them to the Hindi schools). I have been passing them for several months, and receive a variety of greetings—namaste, salaam, good-morning, hello, according to their inclination— and I reply in kind. They are politer up here than down in the town. Could it be the altitude? Possibly. Because down in the town they are politer than down in the valley. And in the valley they are politer (only just) than on the plain.

I believe the highland Scots, are very polite too, except at football matches.

*

Fox-Burn. The name is still on the gate. Of the house only the walls remain.

I take an overgrown path through the deodars and find this knoll with the ruins on it. I can only call it the murder of a house. Its lovely Doric pillars still stand, supporting the sky. A magnificent old horse-chestnut throws its shadow over the broken masonry.

When its owner, an old English (Scottish?) lady died here in the Fifties, there were no heirs, and the property fell into strange hands. The banias and kabaris got hold of the house, and pulled it down, because there was more money to be had from selling the iron beams, the mahogany flooring, the rosewood furnishings. So they stripped the house of everything. They might at least have taken the walls away too, instead of leaving behind this sad reminder of former glory. For a fine house it must have been, the long veranda letting in the afternoon sunshine, the wide lawn lending itself to genteel tea parties and moonlit walks. All that has gone of course, but why should the house have been violated? Now no one can live in it; no one can buy it—for no one is certain who it belongs to—and the walls are so thick, it would take a hundred years of wind and rain to bring them down. Even the cemetery presents a more cheerful sight. Flowers grow between the graves.

12 May

Made Raki's day—had his cycle repaired.
Made Mukesh's day—brought him a cricket bat from Dehra.
Made Mrs Santra's day—said her poems were lovely.
(If, by telling a lie, one can make someone happy, why not tell the damn lie?)

19 May

Prem, Raki, Muki, make it a merry birthday morning, and launch me into my fifties with love and tenderness.

10 June

Went down to Dehra, hoping to find Manohar and repay him for his goodness in caring for me when I was down with a fever in the hotel last month. Too late. He'd left the White House and returned to his village without leaving an address. I'm sorry, friend. Now I shall never be able to thank you properly for your kindness.

28 June

To Dehra again, to see the General, who wants me to write a history of the Military Academy (just twenty-five years old). He evinced great enthusiasm, but wouldn't talk money. Could the army be short of money? Should I do it as a matter of honour? Anyway, I walked all the way back to town (six miles) in the blazing afternoon sun. Authors don't merit army transport.

The evening was pleasant, and I sat on the veranda of the White House (a hotel which was built when I was a boy here), and wrote a poem called *Parts of Old Dehra*:

Parts of old Dehra remain . . . .
A peepul tree I knew
And flying foxes
In a mango grove
And here and there
A moss-encrusted wall
Old bungalows
Gone to seed
And giving way
To concrete slabs.
A garden town's become a city
And the people faceless
As they pass or rather rush
Hell-bent
From place of work
To crowded tenement.
So change must come,
Fields make way for factories,
The trees succumb
To real-estate,
The rivers plunge
Silt-laden
To our doom . . . .
Too late to do a thing
About it now,
For we have grown

Too many,
And the world's no bigger
Than before.
Do-gooders, don't despair!
Nature will repair
Her own, long after
We are dust.

26 July

At fifty, I have received more love than at any other period of my life. Waves of tenderness . . . .

16 August

Raki completes ten. Muki was four earlier this year; Dolly will be three in October. Bright sparks! All power to them.

Julia MacRae Books publish *Tigers Forever,* and I give them a new one, *Earthquake,* which worked quite well, I thought. This is my tenth storybook for children published in the UK. And I have yet to meet my publishers! Odd, how everyone finds it necessary to haunt the offices of editors and publishers, as though a public relations exercise is vital to getting something published.

19 October

'Life can only be understood backwards, but it must be lived forwards.'

(Soren Kierkegaard)

1984

1 January

Refuse to lose.

6 January

Bitterly cold. The snow came in through the bedroom roof.

Not enough money for going away, but at least there's enough for wood and coal. I hate the cold and the snow, but the children love it. Raki, Muki and Dolly in constant high spirits. Snowballing on the road would have touched the heart of Dickens, but right now I would rather be 'bareheaded in the blazing sun at mid-day' like one of Kipling's sunstroke victims.

19 January

Went down to Dehra for the day and had my eyes checked. 'Progressive myopia'. I shall just have to put up with stronger glasses, I suppose.

28 January

Muki completes five, and as usually happens on his birthday, there is a blizzard. The storm raged for two days—howling winds, hail, sleet, snow. In the middle of it Prem had to go out for coal and kerosene oil. Worst weather that I can recall in the hill-station. Sick of it. This is no place for a winter residence. Why do I stay here?

10 March

Gentle weather at last. Peach, plum and apricot trees in blossom. So this is why I stay here.

24 April

What I would really like to write is a children's classic.

Have I written anything approaching one? Some good stories, but they are so easily lost in the flood of literature that spews forth from the presses of the world.

28 April

The feeling of space—of limitless space—can only be experienced by living in the mountains. Or at sea, in the days of the sailing-ships. I think that's why I love sea literature— Masefield, Conrad, Stevenson, Melville . . . . Oddly enough, the mountains haven't inspired many great books. And I don't mean books on mountaineering.

17 May

Depressed all day. Kept thinking of this day, seven years ago, when little Suresh (Raki's younger brother) was taken away so cruelly.

10 June

Monsoon sets in early, but welcome all the same. Perhaps the money drought will break too.

20 June

A name—a lovely face—turn back the years! Forty-five years, to be exact, when I was a small boy in Jamnagar and my father taught English to some of the younger princes and princesses— among them this girl, whose pictures (taken by my father) are still in my old album. She wrote to me after reading an article of mine in a Bombay paper, wanting to know if I was the same boy, 'Mr Bond's son.' I responded, of course. A link with my childhood is so very rare. And besides, I had a crush on her (my first). She'd be about fifty-six now. So long ago—and yet it seems only yesterday.

11 July

Wrote *Getting Granny's Glasses* (3,000 words) in two days; I wrote it with love and tenderness and, I think, with some skill. (It was to be short-listed for the Carnegie Medal the following year; unusual for so short a book.)

20 July

Among the monsoon insects who fly in at the open window after dark, is a very persistent bamboo beetle who must be the incarnation of a *kamikaze* pilot. Wrote a song for him:

A beetle fell into the goldfish bowl,
Hey-ho!
The beetle began to struggle and roll,
Ho-hum!
The window was open, the moon shone bright,

The crickets were singing with all their might,
But a blundering beetle had muddled his flight
And here he was now, in a watery plight,
Having given the goldfish a terrible fright,
Ho-hum, hey-ho!

The beetle swam left, the beetle swam right,
Hum-ho!
Along came myself—I said, 'Lord, what a sight!
That poor old beetle will drown tonight.
Ho-hum.
A beetle is just an insect, I hear,
But what if I fell in a vat full of beer?
I'd be brewed to light lager if no one came near—
(It happened, I'm told, to a man in Ajmer)—
Ho-hum, ho-hum.

With my fingers and thumb
The beetle I seized;
The goldfish were pleased!
The window was open, the moon shone bright,
I flung that beetle far out in the night,
And he bumbled away in a staggering flight,
Ho-hum, hey-ho,
Good night!

8 October

Everyone at JM Books liked *Granny*, and an advance against royalties broke the drought.

Paid rent in advance for a year. But Ivy Cottage looks shaky. Will it come down next monsoon?

MOUNTAINS
ARE KIND
TO WRITERS

*But the
Wind is
Cruel*

In Search of a Winter Garden

IF SOMEONE WERE to ask me to choose between writing an essay on the Taj Mahal or on the last rose of summer, I'd take the rose—even if it was down to its last petal. Beautiful, cold, white marble leaves me—well, just a little cold.

Roses are warm and fragrant, and almost every flower I know, wild or cultivated, has its own unique quality, whether it be subtle fragrance or arresting colour or loveliness of design. Unfortunately, winter has come to the Himalayas, and the hillsides are now brown and dry, the only colour being that of the red sorrel growing from the limestone rocks. Even my small garden looks rather forlorn, with the year's last dark-eyed nasturtium looking every bit like the Lone Ranger surveying the surrounding wilderness from his saddle. The marigolds have dried in the sun, and tomorrow I will gather the seed. The beanstalk that grew rampant during the monsoon is now down to a few yellow leaves and empty bean pods.

'This won't do,' I told myself the other day. 'I must have flowers!'

Prem, who had been down to the valley town of Dehra the previous week, had made me even more restless, because he had spoken of masses of sweet peas in full bloom in the garden of one of the town's public schools. Down in the plains, winter is the best time for gardens, and I remembered my grandmother's house in Dehra, with its long rows of hollyhocks, neatly staked sweet peas, and beds ablaze with red salvia and antirrhinum. Neither Grandmother nor the house are there anymore, but surely there are other beautiful gardens, I mused, and maybe I could visit the school where Prem had seen the sweet peas. It was a long time since I had enjoyed their delicate fragrance.

So I took the bus down the hill, and throughout the two-hour journey I dozed and dreamt of gardens—cottage gardens in the English countryside, tropical gardens in Florida, Mughal gardens in Kashmir, the Hanging Gardens of Babylon!—What had they really been like, I wondered.

And then we were in Dehra, and I got down from the bus and walked down the dusty, busy road to the school Prem had told me about.

It was encircled by a high wall, and, tiptoeing, I could see playing fields and extensive school buildings and, in the far distance, a dollop of colour that *may* have been a garden. Prem's eyesight was obviously better than mine!

I made my way to a wrought-iron gate that would have done justice to a medieval fortress, and found it chained and locked. On the other side stood a tough-looking guard, with a rifle.

'May I enter?' I asked.

'Sorry, sir. Today is holiday. No school today.'

'I don't want to attend classes. I want to see sweet peas.'

'Kitchen is on the other side of the ground.'

'Not green peas. Sweet peas. I'm looking for the garden.'

'I am guard here.'

'*Garden.*'

'No garden, only guard.'

I tried telling him that I was an old boy of the school and that I was visiting the town after a long interval. This was true up to a point, because I had once been admitted to this very school, and after one day's attendance had insisted on going back to my old school. The guard was unimpressed. And perhaps it was poetic justice that the gates were barred to me now.

Disconsolate, I strolled down the main road, past a garage, a cinema, and a row of eating houses and tea shops. Behind the shops there seemed to be a park of sorts, but you couldn't see much of it from the road because of the buildings, the press of people, and the passing trucks and buses. But I found the entrance, unbarred this time, and struggled through patches of overgrown shrubbery until, like Alice after finding the golden key to the little door in the wall, I looked upon a lovely little garden.

There were no sweet peas, and the small fountain was dry. But around it, filling a large circular bed, were masses of bright yellow California poppies.

They stood out like sunshine after rain, and my heart leapt as Wordsworth's must have, when he saw his daffodils. I found myself oblivious to the sounds of the bazaar and the road, just as the people outside seemed oblivious to this little garden. It was as though it had been waiting here all this time, waiting for me to come by and discover it.

I am fortunate. Something like this is always happening to me. As Grandmother often said, 'When one door closes, another door opens.' And while one gate had been closed upon the sweet peas, another had opened on California poppies.

The Words

Observing Ananda weeping, Gautama said,
'O Ananda do not weep. This body of ours
contains within itself the powers which renew
its strength for a time, but also the causes which
lead to its destruction. Is there anything put
together which shall not dissolve?'
Then, turning to his disciples, he said, 'When
I am passed away and am no longer with you,
do not think the Buddha has left you, and is not
still in your midst. You have my words, my
explanations, my laws . . . .' And again, 'Beloved
disciples, if you love my memory, love one another.'
And after another pause he said, 'Beloved,
that which causes life causes also decay
and death. Never forget this. I called you to tell you this.'
These were the last words of Gautama
Buddha, as he stretched himself out and died
under the great sal tree, at Kasinagara.

The Old Lama

I MEET HIM on the road every morning, on my walk up to the Landour post office. He's a lean, old man in a long maroon robe, a Tibetan monk of uncertain age. I'm told he's about eighty-five. But age is really immaterial in the mountains. Some grow old at their mother's breasts, and there are others who do not age at all.

If you are like this old lama, you go on forever. For he is a walking man, and there is no way you can stop him from walking.

The lama in Rudyard Kipling's *Kim*, rejuvenated by the mountain air, strode along with 'steady, driving strokes', leaving his disciple far behind. My lama, older and feebler than Kim's, walks very slowly, with the aid of an old walnut walking-stick. The ferrule keeps coming off the end of the stick, but he puts it back with coal tar, left behind by the road repairers.

He plods and shuffles along. In fact, he's very like the tortoise in the story of the hare and the tortoise. I see him walking past my window, and five minutes later when I start out on the same road, I feel sure of overtaking him halfway up the hill. But invariably I find him standing near the post office when I get there.

He smiles when he sees me. We are always smiling at each other. His English is limited, and I speak absolutely no Tibetan. He knows a few words of Hindi, enough to make his needs known, but that's about all. He is quite happy to converse silently with all the creatures and people who take notice of him on the road.

It's the same walk he takes every morning. At 9 o'clock, if I look out of my window, I can see a line of Tibetan prayer flags fluttering over an old building in the cantonment. He emerges from beneath the flags and starts up the steep road. Ten minutes later he is below my window, and sometimes he stops to sit and rest on my steps, or on a parapet farther along the road. Sooner or later, coming or going, I shall pass him on the road or up near the post office. His eyes will twinkle behind thick-lensed glasses, and he will raise his walking stick slightly in salutation. If I say something to him, he just smiles and nods vigorously in agreement.

An agreeable man.

He was one of those who came to India in 1959, fleeing the Chinese occupation of Tibet. The Dalai Lama found sanctuary in India, and lived here in Mussoorie for a couple of years; many of his followers settled here. A new generation of Tibetans has grown up in the hill-station, and those under thirty years have never seen their homeland.

But for almost all of them, and there are several thousand in this district alone, Tibet is their country, their real home, and they are quick to express their determination to go back when their land is free again.

Even a twenty-year-old girl like Tseten, who has grown up knowing English and Hindi, speaks of the day when she will return to Tibet with her parents. She has given me a painting of Milarepa, the Buddhist monk-philosopher, meditating beneath a fruit-laden peace tree, the eternal snows in the background. This is, perhaps, her vision of the Tibet which she would like to see, some day. Meanwhile, she works as a typist in the office of the Tibetan Homes Foundation.

My old lama will, I am sure, be among the first to return, even if he has to walk all the way over the mountain passes. Maybe that's why he plods up and around this hill every day. He is practicing for the long walk back to Tibet.

Here he is again, pausing at the foot of my steps. It's a cool, breezy morning, and he does not feel the need to sit down.

'*Tashi-tilay!* Good day!' I greet him, in the only Tibetan I know.

'*Tashi-tilay!*' he responds, beaming with delight.

'Will you go back to Tibet one day?' I ask him for the first time.

In spite of his limited Hindi, he understands me immediately, and nods vigorously.

'Soon, soon!' he exclaims, and raises his walking-stick to emphasize his words.

Yes, if the Tibetans are able to return to their country, he will be among the first to go back. His heart is still on that high plateau. And like the tortoise, he'll be there waiting for the young hares to catch up with him.

If he goes, I shall certainly miss him on my walks.

❄

Walk Tall

You stride through the long grass,
Pressing on over fallen pine-needles,
Up the winding road to the mountain-pass:
Small red ant, now crossing a sea
Of raindrops; your destiny
To carry home that single, slender
Cosmos seed,
Waving it like a banner in the sun.

The Night the Roof Blew Off

Looking back at the experience, I suppose it was the sort of thing that should have happened in a James Thurber story, like the dam that burst or the ghost who got in. But I wasn't thinking of Thurber at the time, although a few of his books were among the many I was trying to save from the icy rain and sleet pouring into my bedroom and study.

We have grown accustomed to sudden storms up here at 7,000 feet in the Himalayan foothills, and the old building in which I live has, for over a hundred years, received the brunt of the wind and the rain as they sweep across the hills from the east.

We'd lived in the building for over ten years without any untoward happening. It had even taken the shock of an earthquake without sustaining any major damage: it is difficult to tell the new cracks from the old.

It's a three-storey building, and I live on the top floor with my adopted family—three children and their parents. The roof consists of corrugated tin sheets, the ceiling, of wooden boards. That's the traditional hill-station roof.

Ours had held fast in many a storm, but the wind that night was stronger than we'd ever known it. It was cyclonic in its intensity, and it came rushing at us with a high-pitched eerie wail. The old roof groaned and protested at the unrelieved pressure. It took this battering for several hours while the rain lashed against the windows, and the lights kept coming and going.

There was no question of sleeping, but we remained in bed for warmth and comfort. The fire had long since gone out, the chimney stack having collapsed, bringing down a shower of sooty rain water.

After about four hours of buffeting, the roof could take it no longer. My bedroom faces east, so my portion of the roof was the first to go.

The wind got under it and kept pushing, until, with a ripping, groaning sound, the metal sheets shifted from their moorings, some of them dropping with claps like thunder onto the road below.

So that's it, I thought, nothing worse can happen. As long as the ceiling stays on, I'm not getting out of my bed. We'll pick up the roof in the morning.

Icy water cascading down on my face made me change my mind in a hurry. Leaping from my bed, I found that much of the ceiling had gone too. Water was pouring onto my open typewriter—the typewriter that had been my trusty companion for almost thirty years!—and onto the bedside radio, bed covers, and clothes' cupboard. The only object that wasn't receiving any rain was the potted philodendron, which could have done with a little watering.

Picking up my precious typewriter and abandoning the rest, I stumbled into the front sitting-room (cum library), only to find that a similar situation had developed there. Water was pouring through the wooden slats, raining down on the bookshelves.

By now I had been joined by the children, who had come to rescue me. Their section of the roof hadn't gone as yet. Their parents were struggling to close a window that had burst open, letting in lashings of wind and rain.

'Save the books!' shouted Dolly, the youngest, and that became our rallying cry for the next hour or two.

I have open shelves, vulnerable to borrowers as well as to floods. Dolly and her brother picked up armfuls of books and carried them into their room. But the floor was now awash all over the apartment, so the books had to be piled on the beds. Dolly was helping me gather up some of my manuscripts when a large field rat leapt onto the desk in front of her. Dolly squealed and ran for the door.

'It's all right,' said Mukesh, whose love of animals extends even to field rats. 'He's only sheltering from the storm.'

Big brother Rakesh whistled for our mongrel, Toby, but Toby wasn't interested in rats just then. He had taken shelter in the kitchen, the only dry spot in the house.

At this point, two rooms were practically roofless, and the sky was frequently lighted up for us by flashes of lightning. There were fireworks inside too, as water sputtered and crackled along a damaged electric wire. Then the lights went out altogether, which in some ways made the house a safer place.

Prem, the children's father, is at his best in an emergency, and he had already located and lit two kerosene lamps; so we continued to transfer books, papers, and clothes to the children's room.

We noticed that the water on the floor was beginning to subside a little.

'Where is it going?' asked Dolly, for we could see no outlet.

'Through the floor,' said Mukesh. 'Down to the rooms below.'

He was right, too. Cries of consternation from our neighbours told us that they were now having their share of the flood.

Our feet were freezing because there hadn't been time to put on enough protective footwear, and in any case, shoes and slippers were awash. Tables and chairs were also piled high with books. I hadn't realized the considerable size of my library until that night!

The available beds were pushed into the driest corner of the children's room and there, huddled in blankets and quilts, we spent the remaining hours of the night, while the storm continued to threaten further mayhem.

But then the wind fell, and it began to snow. Through the door to the sitting-room I could see snowflakes drifting through the gaps in the ceiling, settling on picture frames, statuettes and miscellaneous ornaments. Mundane things like a glue-bottle and a plastic doll took on a certain beauty when covered with soft snow. The clock on the wall had stopped and with its covering of snow reminded me of a painting by Salvador Dali. And my shaving-brush looked ready for use!

Most of us dozed off.

I sensed that the direction of the wind had changed, and that it was now blowing from the west; it was making a rushing sound in the trees rather than in what remained of our roof. The clouds were scurrying away.

When the dawn broke, we found the window-panes encrusted with snow and icicles. Then the rising sun struck through the gaps in the ceiling and turned everything to gold. Snow crystals glinted like diamonds on the empty bookshelves. I crept into my abandoned bedroom to find the philodendron looking like a Christmas tree.

Prem went out to find a carpenter and a tin-smith, while the rest of us started putting things in the sun to dry out. And by evening, we'd put much of the roof on again. Vacant houses are impossible to find in Mussoorie, so there was no question of moving.

But it's a much-improved roof now, and I look forward to approaching storms with some confidence!

Garhwal Himalaya

Deep in the crouching mist, lie the mountains.
Climbing the mountains are forests
Of rhododendron, spruce and deodar—
Trees of God, we call them—soughing
In the wind from the passes of Garhwal;
And the snow-leopard moans softly
Where the herdsmen pass, their lean sheep cropping
Short winter grass.
And clinging to the sides of the mountains,
The small stone houses of Garhwal,
Their thin fields of calcinated soil torn
From the old spirit-haunted rocks.
Pale women plough, they laugh at the thunder,
As their men go down to the plains:
Little grows on the beautiful mountains
In the east wind.
There is hunger of children at noon; and yet
There are those who sing of the sunset
And the gods and glories of Himaal,
Forgetting no one eats sunsets.
Wonder, then, at the absence of old men;
For some grow old at their mother's breasts,
In cold Garhwal.

Mountains are Kind to Writers

It's hard to realize that I've been here all these years—twenty-five summers and monsoons and winters and Himalayan springs (there is no spring in the plains)—because, when I look back to the time of my first coming here, it does seem like yesterday.

That probably sums it all up. Time passes, and yet it doesn't pass; people come and go, the mountains remain. Mountains are permanent things. They are stubborn, they refuse to move. You can blast holes out of them for their mineral wealth; or strip them of their trees and foliage, or dam their streams and divert their currents; or make tunnels and roads and bridges; but no matter how hard they try, humans cannot actually get rid of their mountains. That's what I like about them; they are here to stay.

I like to think that I have become a part of this mountain, this particular range, and that by living here for so long, I am able to claim a relationship with the trees, wild flowers, even the rocks that are an integral part of it. Yesterday, at twilight, when I passed beneath a canopy of oak leaves, I felt that I was a part of the forest. I put out my hand and touched the bark of an old tree, and as I turned away, its leaves brushed against my face, as if to acknowledge me.

One day, I thought, if we trouble these great creatures too much, and hack away at them and destroy their young they will simply uproot themselves and march away—whole forests on the move—over the next range and the next, far from the haunts of man. I have seen many forests and green places dwindle and disappear. Now there is an outcry. It is suddenly fashionable to be an environmentalist. That's all right. Perhaps it isn't too late to save the little that's left. They could start by curbing the property developers who have been spreading their tentacles far and wide.

The sea has been celebrated by many great writers—Conrad, Melville, Stevenson, Masefield—but I cannot think of anyone comparable for whom the mountains have been a recurring theme. I must turn to the Taoist poets from old China to find a true feeling for mountains. Kipling does occasionally look to the hills but the Himalayas do not appear to have given rise to any memorable Indian literature, at least not in modern times. By and large, writers have to stay in the plains to make a living. Hill people have their work cut out just trying to wrest a livelihood from their thin, calcinated soil. And as for mountaineers, they climb their peaks and move on, in search of other peaks; they do not take up residence in the mountains.

But to me, as a writer, the mountains have been kind.

They were kind from the beginning, when I left a job in Delhi and rented a small cottage on the outskirts of the hill-station. Today, most hill-stations are rich men's playgrounds, but twenty-five years ago they were places where people of modest means would live quite cheaply. There were few cars and everyone walked about. The cottage was on the edge of the oak and maple forest and I spent eight or nine years in it, most of them happy, writing stories, essays, poems, and books for children. It was only after I came to live in the hills that I began writing for children.

I think this had something to do with Prem's children. He and his wife had taken on the job of looking after the house and all practical matters (I remain helpless with fuses, clogged cisterns, leaking gas cylinders, ruptured water pipes, tin roofs that blow away when there's a storm, and the do-it-yourself world of small-town India). They made it possible for me to write. Their sons Rakesh and Mukesh, and daughter Savitri grew up in Maplewood Cottage and then in other houses when we moved.

Naturally I grew attached to them and became a part of the family, an adopted grandfather. For Rakesh I wrote a story about a cherry tree that had difficulty in growing up; for Mukesh, who liked upheavals, I wrote a story about an earthquake and put him in it; and for Savitri, I wrote rhymes and poems.

One seldom ran short of material. There was a stream at the bottom of the hill and this gave me many subjects in the way of small (occasionally large) animals, wild flowers, birds, insects, ferns. The nearby villages and their good-natured people were of absorbing interest. So were the old houses and old families of the Landour and Mussoorie hill-stations. There were walks into the mountains and along the pilgrim trails, and sometimes I slept at a roadside tea shop or a village school.

'Who goes to the Hills, goes to his Mother.' So wrote Kipling, and he seldom wrote truer words. For, living in the hills was like living in the bosom of a strong, sometimes proud, but always comforting mother. And every time I went away, the homecoming would be more tender and precious. It became increasingly difficult for me to *go* away.

It has not always been happiness and light. There were times when money ran out. Freelancing can be daunting at times, and I never could make enough to buy a house like almost everyone else I know. Editorial doors sometimes close; but when one door closes, another has, for me, almost immediately, miraculously opened. I could perhaps have done a little better living in London, or in Canada like my brother; or even in a city like Bombay. But given the choice, I would not have done differently. When you have received love from people, and the freedom that only the mountains can give, then you have come very near the borders of heaven.

View from the Window

I'm in bed with fever
but the fever's not high.
Beside my bed is a window
and I like looking out at all
that's happening around me.
The cherry leaves are turning a dark green.
On the maple tree, winged seeds spin round and round.
There is fruit on the wild blackberry bushes.
Two mynah birds are building a nest in a hole—
They are very noisy about it.
Bits of grass keep falling on the window sill.
High up in the spruce tree, a hawk-cuckoo calls:
'I slept so well, I slept so well!'
When the hawk-cuckoo is awake, no one else sleeps
That's why it's also known as the fever bird.
A small squirrel climbs on the window sill.
He's been coming every day since I've been ill,
and I give him crumbs from my tray.
A boy on a mule passes by on the rough mountain track.
He sees my face at the window and waves to me.
I wave back to him.
When I'm better I'll ask him to let me ride his mule.

Best of All Windows

Those who advertise rooms or flats to let often describe them as 'room with bath' or 'room with tea and coffee-making facilities'. A more attractive proposition would be 'room with window', for without a view a room is hardly a living place—merely a place of transit.

As an itinerant young writer, I lived in many single-room apartments, or 'bed-sitters' as they were called, and I have to admit that the quality of my life was certainly enhanced if any window looked out on something a little more inspiring than a factory wall or someone's backyard.

We cherish a romantic image of a starving young poet living in a garret and writing odes to skylarks, but, believe me, garrets don't help. For six months in London I lived in a small attic room that had no view at all, except for the roofs of other houses—an endless vista of grey tiles and blackened chimneys, without so much as a proverbial cat to relieve the monotony. I did not write a single ode, for no self-respecting nightingale or lark ever found its way up there.

My next room, somewhere near Clapham Junction, had a 'view of the railway', but you couldn't actually see the railway lines because of the rows of washing that were hung out to dry behind the building.

It was a working-class area, and there were no laundries around the corner. But if you couldn't see the railway, you could certainly hear it. Every time a train thundered past, the building shuddered, and ornaments, crockery, and dishes rattled and rocked as though an earthquake were in progress. It was impossible to hang a picture on the wall; the nail (and with it the picture), fell out after a couple of days. But it reminded me a bit of my Uncle Fred's railway quarters, just near Delhi's main railway station, and I managed to write a couple of train stories while living in this particular room.

Train windows, naturally, have no equal when it comes to views, especially in India, where there's an ever-changing panorama of mountain, forest, desert, village, town, and city—along with the colourful crowds at every railway station.

But good, personal windows—windows to live with—these were to prove elusive for several years. Even after returning to India, I had some difficulty finding the ideal window.

Moving briefly to a small town in northern India, I was directed to the Park View lodging house. There did happen to be a park in the vicinity, but no view of it could be had from my room or, indeed, from any room in the house. But I found, to my surprise, that the bathroom window actually looked out on the park. It provided a fine view! However, there is a limit to the length of time one can spend in the bath, gazing out at palm fronds waving in the distance. So I moved on again.

After a couple of claustrophobic years in New Delhi, I escaped to the hills, fully expecting that I would immediately find rooms or a cottage with windows facing the eternal snows. But it was not to be!

To see the snows I had to walk four miles from my lodgings to the highest point in the hill-station. My window looked out on a high stone rampart, built to prevent the steep hillside from collapsing. True, a number of wild things grew in the wall—bunches of red sorrel, dandelions, tough weeds of various kinds, and, at the base, a large clump of nettles. Now I am sure there are people who can grow ecstatic over nettles, but I am not one of them. I find that nettles sting me at the first opportunity. So I gave my nettles a wide berth.

And then, at last, persistence was rewarded. I found my present abode, a windswept, rather shaky old house on the edge of a spur. My bedroom window opened on to blue skies, mountains striding away into the far distance, winding rivers in the valley below, and, just to bring me down to earth, the

local television tower. Like the Red Shadow in *The Desert Song**
I could stand at my window and sing 'Blue heaven, and you
and I,' even if the only listener was a startled policeman.

The window was so positioned that I could lie on my bed
and look at the sky, or sit at my desk and look at the hills, or
stand at the window and look at the road below.

Which is the best of these views?

Some would say the hills, but the hills never change. Some
would say the road, because the road is full of change and
movement—tinkers, tailors, tourists, salesmen, cars, trucks and
motor-cycles, mules, ponies, and even, on one occasion, an
elephant. The elephant had no business being up here, but I
suppose if Hannibal could take them over the Alps, an attempt
could also be made on the Himalayan passes. (It returned to
the plains the next day.)

The road is never dull, but, given a choice, I'd opt for the
sky. The sky is *never* the same. Even when it's cloudless, the
sky colours are different. The morning sky, the daytime sky,
the evening sky, the moonlit sky, the starry sky, these are all
different skies. And there are almost always birds in the sky—
eagles flying high, mountain swifts doing acrobatics, cheeky
mynah birds meeting under the eaves of the roof, sparrows
flitting in and out of the room at will. Sometimes a butterfly
floats in on the breeze. And on summer nights, great moths
enter at the open window, dazzled by my reading light. I have
to catch them and put them out again, lest they injure
themselves.

When the monsoon rains arrive, the window has to be
closed, otherwise cloud and mist fill the room, and that isn't
good for my books. But the sky is even more fascinating at this
time of the year.

From my desk I can, at this very moment, see the clouds
advancing across the valley, rolling over the hills, ascending the
next rang. Raindrops patter against the window panes, closed
until the rain stops.

* A musical play which was filmed several times; it is also the title song of the
show.

And when the shower passes and the clouds open up, the heavens are a deeper, darker blue. Truly magic casements these . . . for every time I see the sky I am aware of belonging to the universe rather than to just one corner of the earth.

Rain in the Hills

In the hushed silence of the house
when I am quite alone, and my friend, who was here,
has gone, it is very lonely, very quiet,
as I sit in a liquid silence, a silence within,
surrounded by the rhythm of rain
the steady drift
of water on leaves, on lemons, on roof,
drumming on drenched dahlias and window panes,
while the mist holds the house in a dark caress.

As I pause near a window, the rain stops.
And starts again.
And the trees, no longer green but grey,
menace me with their loneliness.

A Knock at the Door

For Sherlock Holmes, it usually meant an impatient client waiting below in the street. For Nero Wolfe, it was the doorbell that rang, disturbing the great man in his orchid rooms. For Poe or Walter de la Mare, that knocking on a moonlit door could signify a ghostly visitor—no one outside!—or, even more mysterious, no one in the house . . . .

Well, clients I have none, and ghostly visitants don't have to knock; but as I spend most of the day at home, writing, I have learnt to live with the occasional knock at the front door. I find doorbells even more startling than ghosts, and ornate brass knockers have a tendency to disappear when the price of brassware goes up; so my callers have to use their knuckles or fists on the solid mahogany door. It's a small price to pay for disturbing me.

I hear the knocking quite distinctly, as the small front room adjoins my even smaller study-cum-bedroom. But sometimes I keep up a pretence of not hearing anything straight away. Mahogany is good for the knuckles! Eventually, I place a pencil between my teeth and holding a sheet of blank foolscap in one hand, move slowly and thoughtfully toward the front door, so that, when I open it, my caller can see that I have been disturbed in the throes of composition. Not that I have ever succeeded in making any one feel guilty about it; they stay as long as they like. And after they have gone, I can get back to listening to my tapes of old Hollywood operettas.

Impervious to both literature and music, my first caller is usually a boy from the village, wanting to sell me his cucumbers or 'France-beans'. For some reason he won't call them French beans. He is not impressed by the accoutrements of my trade. He thrusts a cucumber into my arms and empties the beans on

a coffee-table book which has been sent to me for review.
(There is no coffee-table, but the book makes a good one.) He
is confident that I cannot resist his 'France-beans', even though
this sub-Himalayan variety is extremely hard and stringy.
Actually, I am a sucker for cucumbers, but I take the beans so
I can get the cucumber cheap. In this fashion, authors survive.

The deal done, and the door closed, I decide it's time to do
some work. I start this little essay. If it's nice and gets published,
I will be able to take care of the electricity bill. There's a knock
at the door. Some knocks I recognize, but this is a new one.
Perhaps it's someone asking for a donation. Cucumber in hand,
I stride to the door and open it abruptly only to be confronted
by a polite, smart-looking chauffeur who presents me with a
large bouquet of flowering gladioli!

'With the compliments of Mr B.P. Singh,' he announces,
before departing smartly with a click of the heels. I start
looking for a receptacle for the flowers, as Grandmother's
flower vase was really designed for violets and forget-me-nots.

B.P. Singh is a kind man who had the original idea of
turning his property outside Mussoorie into a gladioli farm. A
bare hillside is now a mass of gladioli from May to September.
He sells them to flower shops in Delhi, but his heart bleeds at
harvesting time.

Gladioli arranged in an ice-bucket, I return to my desk and
am just wondering what I should be writing next, when there
is a loud banging on the door. No friendly knock this time.
Urgent, peremptory, summoning! Could it be the police? And
what have I gone and done? Every good citizen has at least one
guilty secret, just waiting to be discovered! I move warily to the
door and open it an inch or two. It *is* a policeman!

Hastily, I drop the cucumber and politely ask him if I can be
of help. Try to look casual, I tell myself. He has a small packet
in his hands. No, it's not a warrant. It turns out to be a slim
volume of verse, sent over by a visiting DIG of Police, who has
authored it. I thank his emissary profusely, and, after he has
gone, I place the volume reverently on my bookshelf, beside
the works of other poetry-loving policemen. These men of steel,
who inspire so much awe and trepidation in the rest of us, they

too are humans and some of them are poets!

Now it's afternoon, and the knock I hear is a familiar one, and welcome, for it heralds the postman. What would writers do without postmen? They have more power than literary agents. I don't have an agent (I'll be honest and say an agent won't have me), but I do have a postman, and he turns up every day except when there's a landslide.

Yes, it's Prakash the postman who makes my day, showering me with letters, books, acceptances, rejections, and even the occasional cheque. These postmen are fine fellows, they do their utmost to bring the good news from Ghent to Aix.

And what has Prakash brought me today? A reminder: I haven't paid my subscription to the Author's Guild. I'd better send it off, or I shall be a derecognized author. A letter from a reader: would I like to go through her 800-page dissertation on the Gita? Some day, my love . . . . A cheque, a cheque! From Sunflower Books, for nineteen rupees only, representing the sale of six copies of one of my books during the previous year. Never mind. Six wise persons put their money down for my book. No fresh acceptances, but no rejections either. A postcard from Goa, where one of my publishers is taking a holiday. So the post is something of an anti-climax. But I mustn't complain. Not every knock on the door brings gladioli fresh from the fields. Tomorrow's another day, and the postman comes six days a week.

Sounds of the Sea

F OR YEARS I had this large sea-shell, and by putting it to my ear I could hear the distant sob and hiss of the sea—or so I fancied, until this romantic notion was dispelled by twelve-year-old Mukesh, who told me that the same effect could be obtained by holding an empty cup to my ear. He was right, of course. In fact, the cup sounds better than the shell! And for years I'd gone on imagining that the sound of the sea was somehow trapped in my shell . . . . But I still cling to it, for it takes me back to Jamnagar, on the west coast of India, and memories of sea and sand, small steamers and large Arab dhows plying across the Gulf of Kutch.

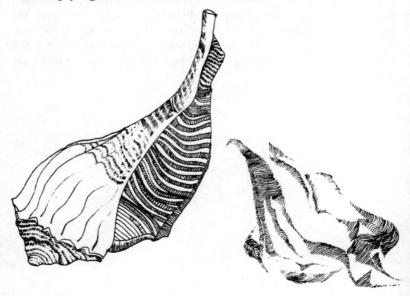

My small hand in my father's, I explored with him the little port's harbour and beach, bringing home shells of considerable variety, and even, on one occasion, a small crab, which lived in a spare bathtub for several days and was forgotten—until a visiting aunt, deciding on a tub-bath after a long train journey, found it keeping her company among the soap-suds. Amidst much clamour and consternation, it was evicted from the house and dropped into a nearby well. But my aunt was convinced that I had deliberately placed it in the tub, and refused to speak to me for the rest of her stay.

A small British steamer was often in port, and my father and I would visit the captain, a good-natured Welshman who gave me chocolates, a great treat in those days, for Jamnagar was too small a place for a Western confectionery shop. I was ready to go to sea with Captain Jenkins, convinced that chocolates were only to be found on tramp steamers.

We left Jamnagar when the Second World War broke out and my father joined the R.A.F. It was to be some ten years before I saw the sea again, for I went to boarding-school in the hills. I was still in my teens, but now bereft of my father, when I set sail from Bombay in the *S. S. Strathnaver*, a beautiful P&O liner, one of a fleet, its sister ships being the *Strathaird* and *Stratheden*. Those were the days of the big passenger liners, before fast air travel put an end to leisurely ocean voyages. It took just over a fortnight to reach Southampton or London, but there was never a dull moment on the voyage. Apart from interesting shipboard acquaintances—the sort of mixed company that gave Somerset Maugham material for his stories—there were also colourful ports of call: Aden, Port Said, Marseilles, Gibraltar. At Marseilles, I decided to miss the coach-tour and instead walk into the town. After three hours of walking along miles and miles of dockland, I finally reached the outskirts of the city—just in time to catch the coach back to the ship!

But later, living in London, I never tired of walking among the docks and wharfs along the Thames, for many of those places were associated with the novels of Dickens, which had inspired me to become a writer. Limehouse, Wapping, Shadwell Stairs, the Mile End Road, the East India Docks, these were all places I knew from *Bleak House*, *Dombey and Son*, and *Our Mutual Friend*. And there was the fog, a thick peasouper, that seemed to have lingered on from the fog that had enveloped the characters and the action in *Bleak House*, setting the tone for that masterpiece. London, I am told, no longer has fogs—they are dispersed by modern and scientific means—and although the air no doubt is cleaner and healthier now, I feel sure some of the magic has gone—along with the East End of old.

From London's dockland to the Channel Islands was a short trip but a considerable change. I lived on the island of Jersey for two years. It had a number of bays and inlets of great charm and beauty, and it was here that I learnt to watch the tides advancing and retreating, and discovered that the tides make different sounds in different places.

Every tide has its own music, and those who live near lonely shores soon learn to recognize the familiar ripple, throb, sob, or sigh. And sometimes the tide comes up from the deep against a steep sand-bank and roars defiance.

The tide-rip which pushes through the Channel Islands off the Norman coast has a smoother thud than most, though it comes from the same Atlantic as the harsher-sounding waters among the Orkneys. The difference may be that the channel tides move through purple waters which have drifted up from sunny Portugal, while the other has a shiver from the coast of Greenland.

The music of sea waters is wonderfully varied. Every bay and headland and strait has its note which the local fisherfolk recognize even in time of dense fog; a note which guides them home or which helps them locate the place for their fishing.

For many years I have been living far from the sea. Sometimes I feel the urge to go down to the sea again, all the way from the Himalayas to Cape Comorin. And maybe I will one day.

Meanwhile, if I wish to listen to the sound of the sea, there's always my sea-shell—or Mukesh's tea-cup.

All my Writing Days

I MUST HAVE been eight or nine when my father gave me a small diary, and I began my first tentative forays as a writer—or wordsmith, as I have sometimes described my calling.

Many of those early diary entries were lists—books read, gramophone records collected, films seen and enjoyed—but even this indulgence was a discipline of sorts and was to stand me in good stead in later years. It made me neat and meticulous, and helped me form the habit of keeping notes and filing away facts: not, perhaps, essential attributes for a writer, but useful ones. Young writers with natural talent are often handicapped by untidy working habits. A friend of mine wrote quite brilliantly but always contrived to lose his manuscripts; he now breeds Angora rabbits.

While at boarding-school in the hill-station of Simla, then the summer capital of British India, I discovered Dickens in the school library and, captivated by David Copperfield, decided I was going to be a writer like David, who was really Charles Dickens. At the age of thirteen I did, in fact, write a short novel, an account of school life—eulogies of my friends, mostly—but it was confiscated by a teacher, who thought I was wasting my time; he may well have been right!

Those schoolboy efforts were, however, not really wasted. I found I could write in a busy classroom, noisy dormitory, a corner of a playing-field; that is, when I really wanted to. As William Saroyan once said, 'All you need is paper,' and there was no shortage of that—empty paper bags, wrappers, pages torn from exercise books, the backs of calendars and school circulars. The wartime paper shortage did not defeat me.

Writing under such conditions, sometimes with a pillow-fight raging around me, was good training too. Later in life I found I was able to write in the crowded compartment of a moving train, or in a room full of children. I love solitude, and there is no pleasure to equal that of writing a poem under a blossoming cherry tree; but I am a compulsive writer, and when I want to put words to paper, I am not fussy about the conditions. Even as I write this piece, a wedding procession is passing along the road beneath my window. It is led by a twelve-piece band, at least six of the instruments being trumpets. The drummers have stationed themselves beneath the window. My cherry tree is a far cry! But the cacophony won't stop me from completing this essay. Play on, band! Blow, blow, thou windy trumpets! Your piercing notes may have loosened the wax in my ears, but my hand remains steady, the words run on . . . .

I had lost my father before I had finished my schooling, and at the age of seventeen I found myself in the English Channel Islands, working in a grocery store, and writing late at night in an attic room provided by an aunt. Most of my relatives were pessimistic about my literary prospects, and there were no literary influences on the islands. Late one winter evening I walked along the sea-front, a lonely figure on the esplanade, while a wind of gale-force blew in from the sea, whipping the salt spray against my face. The tide was in, great waves crashed against the sea wall, sending plumes of water over the ramparts. 'This is it!' I thought. 'These are signs and portents. I must have more resolve. I must not give up!' I decided I would leave for London the next day. I was David Copperfield, of course. The grocery store found itself short of an assistant, while a London travel agency was richer by a very inexperienced clerk. I think it suffered a little because of me, but we both survived, and the first novel got written in fits and starts, at weekends and on holidays. I was bold enough to look for a publisher, and brash enough to find one!

'All glory comes from daring to begin,' said the blurb on the dust cover of my book; but in truth, Glory did nothing of the sort. After receiving a few encouraging reviews, the book all but disappeared from sight. But the advance I received, enabled me to return to India, more determined than ever to be a full-time writer.

In Dehradun, the small town I had known as a boy, I set up 'shop' in a small apartment near the bazaar and made a precarious living from submitting my stories and articles to the English language press in India. But this was one of the happiest periods of my life. Still in my twenties, I was independent, free to write as I pleased, monarch of all I surveyed—which was the local bus stand, a row of small barber shops, and a large tamarind tree dominating everything else. When I passed through Dehra the other day, I was glad to find the tamarind tree still there.

After two years of freelancing, circumstances took me to Delhi and Bombay, but I have always preferred the small-towns of India to its cities. I feel lost in the big city, and too much the stranger in a village. I'm a small town person, and when I came to live in the hills and freelanced again, it was on the outskirts of a small town that I took up residence.

This is, for the most part, a quiet place, and it suits a quiet person. If I want to write on a sunny hill-side or in the shade of a chestnut tree, there is nothing to prevent me from doing so. But I like my desk near the window, close to the busy little road leading to the bazaar. The daily business of life does not distract me.

The marriage procession with its out-of-tune band has moved on. Now a car has stalled on its way up the hill. A truck on the way down cannot get past. There is a furious honking of horns and an exchange of words which are not in the best interests of global harmony. It is all part of my writing life. Blow your horn, charioteer! My hand is steady, and the words run on.

Banyan Tree

I remember you well, old banyan tree
As you stood there, spreading quietly
Over the broken wall.
While adults slept, I crept away
Down the broad veranda steps, around
The outhouse and the melon-ground
Into the shades of afternoon . . . .
Those summers in India no one stirred
Till evening brought the Fever-Bird
And the mem-sahibs rose with the Rising Moon.
In that June of long ago, I roamed
The faded garden of my father's home;
He'd gone away. There was nothing to do
And no one to talk to . . . .
I must have known that giants have few friends
(The great lurk shyly in their private dens)—
And found you hidden by a dark green wall
Of aerial roots.
Intruder in your pillared den, I stood
And shyly touched your old and rugged wood.
And as my hands explored you, giant tree,
I heard you singing!

The Trail to the Bank

LOCAL RESIDENTS HAVE got fed up with offering me lifts on the road to our hilltop bank and post office. They typically drive up the steep road to Landour in third (or is it fourth?) gear, see me plodding along on foot, and out of the goodness of their hearts, stop and open the door for me.

Although I hate to disappoint them, I close the door, thank them profusely, and insist that I am enjoying my walk. They don't believe me, naturally; but with a shrug, the drivers get into gear again and take off, although sometimes they have difficulty getting started, the hill being very steep. As I don't wish to insult them by reaching the bank first, I sit on the parapet wall and make encouraging sounds until they finally take off. Then I renew my leisurely walk up the hill, taking note of the fact that the wild geraniums and periwinkles have begun to flower and that the whistling-thrushes are nesting under the culvert over which those very cars pass every day.

Most people, car drivers anyway, think I'm a little eccentric. So be it. I probably am eccentric! But having come to the Himalayan foot-hills over twenty-five years ago in order to enjoy *walking* among them, I am not about to stop now, just because everyone else has stopped walking. The hills are durable in their attractions, and my legs have proved durable too, so why should we not continue together as before?

The friends who once walked beside me now have their shiny new cars or capacious vans, and seldom emerge from them, unless it be to seek refreshment at some wayside tea shop or cafe.

Now, I'm no fitness freak. I don't jog either. If I did, I would almost certainly miss the latest wildflower to appear on the hillside, and I would not be able to stop awhile and talk to

215

other people on the road—villagers with their milk and vegetables, all-weather postmen, cheeky schoolchildren, inquisitive tourists—or to exchange greetings with cats, dogs, stray cows, and runaway mules.

Runaway mules are friendly creatures except toward their owners. I chat with the owners too, when they come charging up the road. I try to put them in good humour, so as to save the mules from a beating.

Most of the people I have mentioned are walkers from necessity. Those who walk for pleasure grow fewer by the day.

I don't mean long-distance trekkers or high altitude climbers, who are almost professional in their approach to roads and mountains. I mean people such as myself who are not great athletes but who enjoy sauntering through the woods on a frosty morning, leaving the main road and slithering downhill into a bed of ferns, or following a mountain stream until you reach the small spring in the rocks where it begins . . . . But, no—everyone must have a destination in mind, for this is the age of destinations, be it the Taj Mahal, the casino at Cannes, or the polar icecap. I glanced at a bestselling book of records the other day, and my eye lighted upon an entry stating that somebody's grandmother had knitted a scarf that was over twenty miles long. Where was it going, I wondered, and who would be wearing it? The book didn't say. It was just another destination, another 'first' to be recorded.

Personally I prefer people who come in second. I feel safer with them.

It takes a car less than five minutes up the hill to get to the bank. It takes me roughly twenty-five minutes. But there is never a dull minute. Apart from having interesting animal and human encounters, there are the changes that occur almost daily on the hill slopes: the ferns turning from green to gold, the Virginia creepers becoming a dark crimson, horse chestnuts falling to the ground.

On today's walk I spot a redstart, come down early from higher altitudes to escape the snow. He whistles cheerfully in a medlar tree. Wild ducks are flying south. There they go, high over the valley, heading for the lakes and marshlands.

If there's no one on the road, and I feel like a little diversion, I can always sing. I don't sing well, but there's no one to hear me except for a startled woodpecker, so I can go into my Nelson Eddy routine, belting out the songs my childhood gramophone taught me. 'Tramp, Tramp, Tramp,' 'Stouthearted Men,' 'Song of the Open Road!' No one writes marching songs now, so I have to rely on the old ones.

Above me the blue sky, around me the green forest, below me the dusty plains.

Presently I am at Char-Dukaan—'Four Shops'—and the bank and post office.

Letters posted, I enter the bank, to be greeted effusively by the manager, Vishal Ohri—not because I have come to make a large deposit, but because he is that rarity among bank managers, a nature lover! When he learns that I have just seen the first redstart of the winter, he grows excited and insists that I take him to it. As we are nearing the office tea break, he sets off with me down the road and, to our mutual satisfaction and delight, is still in the medlar tree, putting on a special performance seemingly for our benefit.

The manager returns to his office, happy to be working at this remote hilltop branch. Both staff and customers will find him the most understanding and sympathetic of managers today, for has he not just seen the first white-capped redstart to fly into Landour for the winter? That's as good a 'first' as any in those books of records.

As long as there are nature-loving bank managers, I muse on my way home, there's still hope for this little old world. And for bank depositors, too!

Hill-Station

There is nothing to keep me here,
Only these mountains of silence
And the gentle reserve of shepherds and woodmen
Who know me as one who
Walks among trees.

Madman, misanthropist? They make
Their guesses, smile and pass slowly
Down the steep path near the cottage. There is nothing
To keep me here, walking
Among old trees.

Where the Grass Grows Greener

Early in summer the grass on the hills is still a pale yellowish green, tinged with brown, and that is how it remains until the monsoon rains bring new life to everything that subsists on the stony Himalayan soil. And then, for four months, the greens are deep and dark and emerald bright.

But the other day, taking a narrow path that left the dry Mussoorie ridge to link up with Pari Tibba, I ran across a patch of lush green grass, and I knew there had to be water there.

The grass was soft and springy, spotted with the crimson of small, wild strawberries. Delicate maidenhair, my favourite fern, grew from a cluster of moist, glistening rocks. Moving the ferns a little, I discovered the spring, a freshet of clear sparkling water.

I never cease to wonder at the tenacity of water—its ability to make its way through various strata of rock, zigzagging, back-tracking, finding space, cunningly discovering faults and fissures in the mountain, and sometimes travelling underground for great distances before emerging into the open. Of course, there's no stopping water. For no matter how tiny that little trickle, it has to go somewhere!

Like this little spring. At first I thought it was too small to go anywhere, that it would dry up at the edge of the path. Then I discovered that the grass remained soft and green for some distance along the verge, and that there was moisture beneath the grass. This wet stretch ended abruptly; but, on looking further, I saw that it continued on the other side of the path, after briefly going underground again.

I decided to follow its fortunes as it disappeared beneath a tunnel of tall grass and bracken fern. Slithering down a stony slope, I found myself in a small ravine, and there I discovered that my little spring had grown, having been joined by the waters of another spring bubbling up from beneath a patch of primroses.

A short distance away, a spotted forktail stood on a rock, surveying this marriage of the waters. His long, forked tail moved slowly up and down. He paid no attention to me, being totally absorbed in the movements of a water spider. A swift peck, and the spider vanished, completing the bird's breakfast. Thirsty, I cupped my hands and drank a little water. So did the forktail. We had a perennial supply of pure *aqua minerale* all to ourselves!

There was now a rivulet to follow, and I continued down the ravine until I came to a small pool that was fed not only by my brook, (I was already thinking of it as my very own!) but also by a little cascade of water coming down from a rocky ledge. I climbed a little way up the rocks and entered a small cave, in which there was just enough space for crouching down. Water dripped and trickled off its roof and sides. And most wonderful of all, some of these drops created tiny rainbows, for a ray of sunlight had struck through a crevice in the cave roof making the droplets of moisture radiant with all the colours of the spectrum.

When I emerged from the cave, I saw a pair of pine martins drinking at the pool. As soon as they saw me, they were up and away, bounding across the ravine and into the trees.

The brook was now a small stream, but I could not follow it much further, because the hill went into a steep decline and the water tumbled over large, slippery boulders, becoming a waterfall and then a noisy little torrent as it sped toward the valley.

Climbing up the sides of the ravine to the spur of Pari Tibba, I could see the distant silver of a meandering river, and I knew my little stream was destined to become part of it; and that the river would be joined by another that could be seen slipping over the far horizon, and that their combined waters would enter the great Ganga, or Ganges, further downstream.

This mighty river would, in turn, wander over the rich alluvial plains of northern India, finally debouching into the ocean near the Bay of Bengal.

And the ocean, what was it but another droplet in the universe, in the greater scheme of things? No greater than the glistening drop of water that helped start it all, where the grass grows greener around my little spring on the mountain.

❊

Silent Birth

When the earth gave birth to this tree,
There came no sound:
A green shoot thrust
In silence from the ground.
Our births don't come so quiet—
Most lives run riot—
But the bud opens silently,
And flower gives way to fruit.
So must we search
For the stillness within the tree,
The silence within the root.

Better to Have a Bird in a Bush

THE THING I like most about shrubs and small bushes is that they are about my size or thereabouts. I can meet them on equal terms. Most trees grow tall, they overtake us after a few years, and we find ourselves looking up to them with a certain amount of awe and deference. And so we should.

A bush, on the other hand, may have been in the ground a long time—thirty or forty years or more—while continuing to remain a bush, man-sized and approachable. A bush may spread sideways or gain in substance, but it seldom towers over you. This means that I can be on intimate terms with it, know its qualities—of leaf, bud, flower, and fruit—and also its inhabitants, be they insects, birds, small mammals, or reptiles.

Of course, we know that bushes are ideal for binding the earth together and preventing erosion. In this respect they are just as important as trees. Every monsoon I witness landslides all about me, but I know the hillside just above my cottage is well-knit, knotted and netted, by bilberry and raspberry, wild jasmine, dog-rose and bramble, and other shrubs, vines, and creepers.

I have made a small bench in the middle of this civilized wilderness. And sitting here, I can look down on my own roof, as well as sideways and upward, into a number of bushes, teeming with life throughout the year. This is my favourite place. No one can find me here, unless I call out and make my presence known. The buntings and sparrows, 'grown accustomed to my face' and welcoming the grain I scatter for them, flit about near my feet. One of them, bolder than the rest, alights on my shoe and proceeds to polish his beak on the leather. The sparrows are here all the year round. So are the whistling-thrushes, who live in the shadows between house and hill, sheltered by a waterwood bush, so-called because it likes cool, damp places.

Summer brings the fruit-eating birds, for, now the berries are ripe, a pair of green pigeons, rare in these parts, scramble over the branches of a hawthorn bush, delicately picking off the fruit. The raspberry bush is raided by bands of finches and greedy yellow-bottomed bulbuls. A flock of bright green parrots comes swooping down on the medlar tree, but they do not stay for long. Taking flight at my approach, they wheel above, green and gold in the sunlight, and make for the plum trees further down the road.

The kingera, a native Himalayan shrub similar to the bilberry, attracts small boys as well as birds. On their way to and from school, the boys scramble up the hillside and help themselves to the small sweet and sour berries. Then, lips stained purple, they go their merry way. The birds return.

Other inhabitants of this shrub-land include the skink, a tiny lizard-like reptile, quite harmless. It emerges from its home among stones or roots to sun itself or drink from a leaf-cup of water. I have to protect these skinks from a large prowling tabby cat who thinks the hillside and everything on it belongs to him. From my bench, I can see him move stealthily around the corner of my roof. He has his eye on the slow-moving green pigeons, I am sure. I shall have to watch out for him.

There wouldn't be much point in encouraging the birds to visit my bushes if the main beneficiary is to be that handsome, but singleminded cat!

There are flowering shrubs, too—a tangle of dog-roses, the wild yellow jasmine, a buddleia popular with honey bees, and a spreading mayflower which today is covered with small saffron-winged butterflies.

The grass, straw-yellow in winter, is now green and sweet, sprinkled with buttercups and clover. I can abandon the bench and lie on the grass, studying it at close quarters while repeating Whitman's lines:

> *A child said 'What is the grass?' fetching it to me with*
> *full hands.*
> *How could I answer the child? I do not know what it is*
> *any more than he.*

I am no wiser, either, but grass is obviously a good thing, providing a home for crickets and ladybirds and other small creatures. It wouldn't be much fun living on a planet where grass could not grow.

That cat agrees with me. He is flat on his stomach on the grass, inching closer to one of those defenceless little skinks. He has decided that a skink in hand is worth two birds in a bush. I get to my feet, and the cat runs away.

The green pigeons have also flown away. The smaller birds remain where they are; they know they are too swift for the prowler. I return to my bench and watch the finches and coppersmiths arrive and depart.

You might call my shrubbery an arrival and departure lounge for small birds, but they are also free to take up residence if they wish. Their presence adds sweetness to my life. A bush at hand is good for many a bird!

Coaxing a Garden from Himalayan Soil

I WOULDN'T GO so far as to say that a garden is the answer to all problems, but its amazing how a little digging and friendly dialogue with the good earth can help reactivate us when we grow sluggish.

Whenever I'm stuck in the middle of a story or an essay, I go into my tiny hillside garden and get down to the serious business of transplanting or weeding or pruning or just plucking off dead blooms, and in no time at all I'm struck with a notion of how to proceed with the stalled story, reluctant essay, or unresolved poem.

Not all gardeners are writers, but you don't have to be a writer to benefit from the goodness of your garden. Baldev, who heads a large business corporation in Delhi, tells me that he wouldn't dream of going to his office unless he'd spent at least half an hour in his garden that morning. If you can start the day by looking at the dew on your antirrhinums, he tells me, you can face the stormiest of board meetings.

Or take Cyril, an old friend.

When I met him, he was living in a small apartment on the first floor of a building that looked over a steep, stony precipice. The house itself appeared to be built on stilts, although these turned out to be concrete pillars. Altogether an ugly edifice. 'Poor Cyril,' I thought. 'There's no way *he* can have a garden.'

I couldn't have been more wrong. Cyril's rooms were surrounded by a long veranda that allowed in so much sunlight and air, resulting in such a profusion of leaf and flower, that at first I thought I was back in one of the greenhouses at Kew Gardens, where I used to wander during a lonely sojourn in London.

Cyril found a chair for me among the tendrils of a climbing

ivy, while a coffee-table materialized from behind a plant. By the time I had recovered enough from taking in my arboreal surroundings, I discovered that there were at least two other guests—one concealed behind a tree-sized philodendron, the other apparently embedded in a pot of begonias.

Cyril, of course, was an exception. We cannot all have sunny verandas; nor would I show the same tolerance as he does towards the occasional caterpillar on my counterpane. But he was a happy man until his landlord, who lived below, complained that water was cascading down through the ceiling.

'Fix the ceiling,' said Cyril, and went back to watering his plants. It was the end of a beautiful tenant-landlord relationship.

So let us move on to the washer-woman who lives down the road, a little distance from my own abode. She and her family live at the subsistence level. They have one square meal at midday, and they keep the leftovers for the evening. But the steps to their humble quarters are brightened by geraniums potted in large tin cans, all ablaze with several shades of flower.

Hard as I try, I cannot grow geraniums to match hers. Does she scold her plants the way she scolds her children? Maybe I'm not firm enough with my geraniums. Or has it something to do with the washing? Anyway, her abode certainly looks more attractive than some of the official residences here in Mussoorie, India.

Some gardeners like to specialize in particular flowers, but specialization has its dangers. My friend, Professor Saili, an ardent admirer of the nature poetry of William Wordsworth, decided he would have his own field of nodding daffodils, and planted daffodil bulbs all over his frontyard. The following spring, after much waiting, he was rewarded by the appearance of a solitary daffodil that looked like a railway passenger who had gotten off at the wrong station. This year he is specializing in 'easy-to-grow' French marigolds. They grow easily enough in France, I'm sure; but the professor is discovering that they are stubborn growers on our stony Himalayan soil.

Not everyone in this Indian hill-station has a lovely garden. Some palatial homes and spacious hotels are approached through forests of weeds, clumps of nettle, and dead or dying rose bushes. The owners are often plagued by personal problems that prevent them from noticing the state of their gardens. Loveless lives, unloved gardens.

On the other hand, there was Annie Powell, who, at the age of ninety, was up early every morning to water her lovely garden. Watering-can in hand, she would move methodically from one flower-bed to the next, devotedly giving each plant a sprinkling. She said she loved to see leaves and flowers sparkling with fresh water; it gave her a new lease on life every day.

And there were my maternal grandparents, whose home in Dehra in the valley was surrounded by a beautiful, well-kept garden. How I wish I had been old enough to prevent that lovely home from passing into other hands. But no one can take away our memories.

Grandfather looked after the orchard, Grandmother looked after the flower garden. Like all people who have lived together for many years, they had the occasional disagreement.

Grandfather would proceed to sulk on a bench beneath the jack-fruit tree while, at the other end of the garden, Grandmother would start clipping a hedge with more than her usual vigour. Silently, imperceptibly, they would make their way toward the centre of the garden, where the flower-beds gave way to a vegetable patch. This was neutral ground. My cousins and I looked on like UN observers. And there among the cauliflowers, conversation would begin again, and the quarrel would be forgotten. There's nothing like home-grown vegetables for bringing two people together.

Red roses for young lovers. French beans for longstanding relationships!

Where Rivers Meet

IT'S A FUNNY thing, but long before I arrive at a place I can usually tell whether I am going to like it or not.

Thus, while I was still some twenty miles from the town of Pauri, I felt it was not going to be my sort of place; and sure enough, it wasn't. On the other hand, while Nandprayag was still out of sight, I knew I was going to like it. And I did.

Perhaps it's something on the wind—emanations of an atmosphere—that are carried to me well before I arrive at my destination. I can't really explain it, and no doubt it is silly to make judgements in advance. But it happens and I mention the fact for what it's worth.

As for Nandprayag, perhaps I'd been there in some previous existence, I felt I was nearing home as soon as we drove into this cheerful roadside hamlet, some little way above the Nandakini's confluence with the Alakananda river. A *prayag* is a meeting place of two rivers, and as there are many rivers in the Garhwal Himalayas, all linking up to join either the Ganga or the Jamuna, it follows that there are numerous *prayags*, in themselves places of pilgrimage as well as wayside halts *en route* to the higher Hindu shrines at Kedarnath and Badrinath. Nowhere else in the Himalayas are there so many temples, sacred streams, holy places and holy men.

Some little way above Nandprayag's busy little bazaar, is the tourist rest-house, perhaps the nicest of the tourist lodges in this region. It has a well-kept garden surrounded by fruit trees and is a little distance from the general hubbub of the main road.

Above it is the old pilgrim path, on which you walked. Just over twenty years ago, if you were a pilgrim intent on finding salvation at the abode of the gods, you travelled on foot all the way from the plains, covering about 200 miles in a couple of months. In those days people had the time, the faith and the endurance. Illness and misadventure often dogged their footsteps, but what was a little suffering if at the end of the day they arrived at the very portals of heaven? Some did not survive to make the return journey. Today's pilgrims may not be lacking in devotion, but most of them do expect to come home again.

Along the pilgrim path are several handsome old houses, set among mango trees and the fronds of the papaya and banana. Higher up the hill the pine forests commence, but down here it is almost sub-tropical. Nandprayag is only about 3,000 feet above sea level—a height at which the vegetation is usually quite lush provided there is protection from the wind.

In one of these double-storeyed houses lives Mr Devki Nandan, scholar and recluse. He welcomes me into his house and plies me with food till I am close to bursting. He has a great love for his little corner of Garhwal and proudly shows me his collection of clippings concerning this area. One of them is from a travelogue by Sister Nivedita—an Englishwoman, Margaret Noble, who became an interpreter of Hinduism to the West. Visiting Nandprayag in 1928, she wrote:

> Nandprayag is a place that ought to be famous for its beauty and order. For a mile or two before reaching it we had noticed the superior character of the agriculture and even some careful gardening of fruits and vegetables. The peasantry also, suddenly grew handsome, not unlike the Kashmiris. The town itself is new, rebuilt since the Gohna flood, and its temple stands far out across the fields on the shore of the Prayag. But in this short time a wonderful energy has been at work on architectural carvings, and the little place is full of gemlike beauties. Its temple is dedicated to Naga Takshaka. As the road crosses the river, I noticed two or three old Pathan tombs, the only traces of Mohammedanism that we had seen north of Srinagar in Garhwal.

Little has changed since Sister Nivedita's visit, and there is still a small and thriving Pathan population in Nandprayag. In fact, when I called on Mr Devki Nandan, he was in the act of sending out Id greetings to his Muslim friends. Some of the old graves have disappeared in the debris from new road cuttings: an endless business, this road-building. And as for the beautiful temple described by Sister Nivedita. I was sad to learn that it had been swept away by a mighty flood in 1970, when a cloudburst and subsequent landslide on the Alakananda resulted in great destruction downstream.

Mr Nandan remembers the time when he walked to the small hill-station of Pauri to join the old Messmore Mission School, where so many famous sons of Garhwal received their early education. It would take him four days to get to Pauri. Now it is just four hours by bus. It was only after the Chinese invasion of 1962 that there was a rush of road-building in the hill districts of northern India. Before that, everyone walked and thought nothing of it!

Sitting alone that same evening in the little garden of the rest-house, I heard innumerable birds break into song. I did not see any of them, because the light was fading and the trees were dark, but there was the rather melancholy call of the hill dove, the insistent ascending trill of the koel, and much shrieking, whistling and twittering that I was unable to assign to any particular species.

Now, once again, while I sit on the lawn surrounded by zinnias in full bloom, I am teased by that feeling of having been here before, on this lush hillside, among the pomegranates and oleanders. Is it some childhood memory asserting itself? But as a child I never travelled in these parts.

True, Nandprayag has some affinity with parts of the Doon valley before it was submerged by a tidal wave of humanity. But in the Doon there is no great river running past your garden. Here there are two, and they are also part of this feeling of belonging. Perhaps in some former life I did come this way, or maybe I dreamed about living here. Who knows? Anyway, mysteries are more interesting than certainties.

Presently the room-boy joins me for a chat on the lawn. He

is in fact running the rest-house in the absence of the manager. A coach-load of pilgrims is due at any moment but until they arrive the place is empty and only the birds can be heard. His name is Janakpal and he tells me something about his village on the next mountain, where a leopard has been carrying off goats and cattle. He doesn't think much of the conservationists' law protecting leopards: nothing can be done unless the animal becomes a man-eater!

A shower of rain descends on us, and so do the pilgrims. Janakpal leaves me to attend to his duties. But I am not left alone for long. A youngster with a cup of tea appears. He wants me to take him to Mussoorie or Delhi. He is fed up, he says, with washing dishes here.

'You are better off here,' I tell him sincerely. 'In Mussoorie you will have twice as many dishes to wash. In Delhi, ten times as many.'

'Yes, but there are cinemas there,' he says, 'and television, and videos.' I am left without an argument. Birdsong may have charms for me but not for the restless dish-washer in Nandprayag.

The rain stops and I go for a walk. The pilgrims keep to themselves but the locals are always ready to talk. I remember a saying (and it may have originated in these hills), which goes: 'All men are my friends. I have only to meet them.' In these hills, where life still moves at a leisurely and civilized pace, one is constantly meeting them.

After the Monsoon

Toward the end of the year, those few monsoon clouds that still linger over the Himalayas are no longer burdened with rain and are able to assume unusual shapes and patterns, chasing each other across the sky and disappearing in spectacular sunset formations.

I have always found this to be the best time of the year in the hills. The sun-drenched hillsides are still an emerald green; the air is crisp, but winter's bite is still a month or two away; and for those who still like to take to the open road on foot, there are springs, streams, and waterfalls tumbling over rocks that remain dry for most of the year. The lizard that basked on a sun-baked slab of granite last May is missing, but in his place the spotted forktail trips daintily among the boulders in a stream; and the strident sound of the cicadas is gradually replaced by the gentler trilling of the crickets and grasshoppers.

Now, more than at any other time of the year, the wildflowers come into their own.

The hillside is covered with flowers and ferns. Sprays of wild ginger, tangles of clematis, flat clusters of yarrow and lady's mantle. The datura grows everywhere with its graceful white balls and prickly fruits. And the wild woodbine provides the stems from which the village boys make their flutes.

Aroids are plentiful and attract attention by their resemblance to snakes with protruding tongues—hence the popular name, cobra lily. This serpent's tongue is a perfect landing stage for flies, who, crawling over the male flowers in their eager search for the liquor that lies at the base of the spike, succeed in fertilizing the female flowers as they proceed.

One of the more spectacular cobra lilies, which rejoices in the name *Sauromotum Guttatum*—ask your nearest botanist what that means—bears a solitary leaf and purple spathe. When the seeds form, it withdraws the spike underground. And when the rains are over and the soil is not too damp, sends it up again covered with scarlet berries. In the opinion of the hill folk, the appearance of the red spike is more to be relied on as a forecast of the end of the monsoon than any meteorological expertise. Up here on the ranges that fall between the Jamuna and the Bhagirathi (known as the Rawain) we can be perfectly sure of fine weather a fortnight after that fiery spike appears.

But it is the commelinea, more than any other Himalayan flower, that takes my breath away. The secret is in its colour; a pure pristine blue that seems to reflect the deepest blue of the sky. Toward the end of the rains it appears as if from nowhere, graces the hillside for the space of about two weeks, and disappears again until the following monsoon.

When I see the first commelinea, I stand dumb before it, and the world stands still while I worship. So absorbed do I become in its delicate beauty that I begin to doubt the reality of everything else in the world.

But only for a moment. The blare of a truck's horn reminds me that I am still lingering on the main road leading out of the hill-station. A cloud of dust and a blast of diesel fumes are further indication that reality takes many different forms, assailing all my senses at once! Even my commelinea seems to shrink from the onslaught. But as it is still there, I take heart and leave the highway for a lesser road.

Soon I have left the clutter of the town behind. What did Aunt Ruby say the other day? 'Stand still for five minutes, and they will build a hotel on top of you.'

Wasn't it Lot's wife who was turned into a pillar of salt when she looked back at the doomed city that had been her home? I have an uneasy feeling that I will be turned into a pillar of cement if I look back, so I plod on along the road to Devasari, a kindly village in the valley. It will be some time before the 'developers' and big-money boys get here, for no one will go to live where there is no driveway!

A tea shop beckons. How would one manage in the hills without these wayside tea shops? Miniature inns, they provide food, shelter, and even lodging to dozens at a time.

I tackle some buns that have a pre-Independence look about them. They are rock hard, to match the environment, but I manage to swallow some of the jagged pieces with the hot sweet tea.

There is a small shrine here, right in front of the tea shop. It is no more than a slab of rock daubed with vermilion, strewn with offerings of wildflowers. Hinduism comes closest to being a nature religion. Rivers, rocks, trees, plants, animals, and birds all play their part, both in mythology and in everyday worship. This harmony is most evident in remote places like this, and I hope it does not lose its unique character in the ruthless urban advance.

The Road to Anjani Sain

F OG, MIST, CLOUD, rain, and mildew—these were the things the British must have looked for when selecting suitable sites for the hill-stations they set up in the Himalayan foothills 150 years ago: Simla, Mussoorie, Darjeeling, Dalhousie, Nainital, all soggy with monsoon or winter mist and dripping oaks and deodars. The climate must have reminded them of their homes on the English moors or the Scottish highlands.

I have survived all that some thirty mountain monsoons that have been thrown at me; and having gone through the annual ritual of wiping the mildew from my books and a certain green fungus from my one and only suit, I decided to leave cloud country behind for a few days and be the guest of Cyril Raphael, at the Bhuvneshwari Mahila Ashram (a social service organization), at Anjani Sain in Tehri-Garhwal.

Pine country this, dry and bracing, with the scent of pine resin in the air. I have always thought 5,000 to 6,000 feet a healthier altitude to live at, but perhaps I'm prejudiced, having been born in Kasauli, which is pine rather than deodar country. Anjani Sain is about the same height and gets the sun all day. Given adequate food and pure water, it's a healthy place to live. Contrary to what most people think, Garhwal is not a poverty-stricken area. Almost everyone has a bit of land and does at least have the traditional *do-roti* for sustenance, which is more than can be said for the urban unemployed in other parts of northern India. But medical facilities are certainly lacking.

This area has always been known as Khas-patti, probably because it was special in several ways—climate-wise and probably economy-wise too. Down in the flat valley, there are green fields and even mango trees, the descent to lower altitudes being quite sudden in these parts. The small Anjani Sain bazaar, with its single bank, post office, and chemist's shop, shimmers in the noonday sun; it looks like a set for the gunfight at the OK Corral. But this is, generally, a peaceful area.

At the ashram, I am in time for an early lunch—thick rotis made from *mandwa* (millets)—two of these are more than enough for me! Endless glasses of milky tea will see me through till supper time.

Towering over Anjani Sain, and blessing all those who live or pass beneath, is the Chanderbadni temple, dedicated to one of the incarnations of the goddess Parvati. As this is not one of the main pilgrim routes, the temple does not get as many visitors as some of the other sacred shrines in the hills. Below the Chanderbadni peak is a rest-house, for those who wish to break their journey here.

Anjani Sain lies midway between Tehri and Devprayag—a two-hour bus ride from either place. I came via Tehri, the road climbing steeply above the hot, dusty town that is destined to be submerged by the waters of the Tehri Dam. The dam should have been ready by now, but having been the subject of a great deal of controversy, work on it has progressed in fits and starts.

I am told that this entire region is 'eco-fragile', one of those words bandied around at seminars all over the world. Well, I am not an expert in these matters, (and who is, I wonder?) but I should think most of our earth is 'eco-fragile', having had to put up with hundreds of thousands of years of human civilization.

Do we stop all development in the name of preserving the environment? Or do we move on regardless? *Proceed with caution* would be the rational person's answer. But are human beings really rational?

Old Tehri was no beauty spot, and New Tehri (growing rapidly above it), is even uglier; from a distance it looks like a giant cemetery.

When the architecture of sub-urban Delhi is brought to the hills, what is there to say? You just look the other way.

Fortunately the defaced mountain is soon left behind, and as it slips out of sight and we ascend into the pine regions, the eye is soothed by the pretty, slate-covered houses of the villages and their little gardens ablaze with marigolds and yellow and bronze chrysanthemums. Chrysanthemums love this climate. Down in the fields there are patches of crimson *cholai* (amaranth) interspersed with the fresh green of young wheat.

And here be leopards! My companion tells me of one that strolls down the motor road every evening, forcing the local bus to go around him. His presence also accounts for the absence of stray dogs.

Suddenly in the distance I see what at first glance appears to be a cloud or a large white sailing ship. On approaching, it turns out to be the freshly white-washed buildings of the Bhuvneshwari Mahila Ashram, clinging to the steep slopes of the mountain.

Here, for two or three days, I find rest and sustenance. The manifold activities of the ashram, (directed mainly towards the welfare of widows and small children) are there for all to see, and I recall the relief work undertaken by its young field workers after the Uttarkashi earthquake last year—they had rushed to the area before the government agencies could swing into action.

However, as a social worker I am somewhat inept. I am just a frazzled old writer who never made it to the bestseller lists and who now seeks a refuge from the all-pervasive clutter of tourism that makes ordinary life almost impossible in our hill-stations.

I hope the land-grabbers and the real estate 'developers' never get this far. They are welcome to their malls and artificial lakes and concrete parks. Just so long as I am free to escape from it all, to sit here at Anjani Sain contemplating a large white rose in Cyril's garden, while the rest of the world watches video.

The Fern

The slender maidenhair fern grows firm on a rock
While all around her the water swirls and chatters
And then disappears in a rush
Down to the bottom of the hill.
When I'm surrounded by troubled waters, Lord,
Let me find within a rock to cling to,
And give me the quiet patience of the maidenhair
Who has learned to live with the rock.

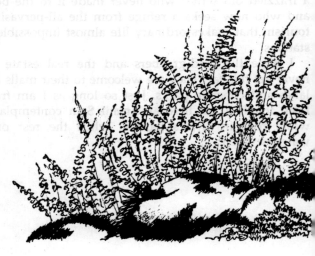

TIME
TO CLOSE
THE WINDOW

The Mountains Remain

Epilogue

THIS RECORD OF my years in the hills is based on journals, notebooks, diary entries and personal essays. That's what life is really like—episodic, full of highs and lows and some fairly dull troughs in between. Life is not a novel; it does not have the organization of a novel. People are not characters in a play; they refuse to conform to the exigencies of a plot or a set of scenes. Some people become an integral part of our lives; others are ships that pass in the night. Short stories, in fact.

My life can really be divided into two sections. The first thirty years, when I was fairly restless and on the move, never long in one place or with one set of friends; and the second thirty years, almost entirely spent in the mountains, when I became about as fixed and permanent as the horse-chestnut that I see from my window.

Only the other day, an old friend, Abha Saili, wife of the daffodil-growing professor, said, 'Ruskin we've known you for thirty years, but we know nothing about you *before* you came here . . . .

I like to pretend that my earlier life was something of a mystery, but in truth it was fairly mundane—boarding-school life, a few years abroad, then working in an office in Delhi—and no, I did not get married, in spite of the rumours that come back to me from time to time!

There were only two occasions in my life when I came really close to getting married. Once in London, when I was twenty-one and infatuated with a very sweet and pretty Vietnamese girl, who promised me her hand until she met a rich American and found his signature more attractive than mine. And the second time, when I met a nurse from Ferozepur, who made it her business to take charge of me for several months. She was

a fine, strapping girl, but I think I would have felt *sat upon* (literally, too) if I had been yoked to her for life.

Perhaps I should have married Miss Bun. But I don't see myself writing stories in the back of a beauty parlour.

I am all for people getting married, for I think the human race should continue (in spite of its obvious limitations), but I think my own contribution to the quality of life must come through the written word and, of course, any encouragement I can give to others in their struggle for survival.

I am not a recluse. Those who have skimmed through these pages will know that for the past twenty-five years I have been living with Prem and his family, or they with me, I am not sure at this point how to put it, except that we are an interdependent and tightly-knit family unit. On with the family! . . . but I also cherish my privacy and my small study-cum-bedroom, facing the morning sun, where I live amongst my books, papers, typewriter and potted plants. The ivy on my wall, the fern on my desk, the lemon geranium, all receive my close attention.

As a child, I hated seeing my parents quarrel, time and time again, until they separated and went their different ways. My father looked after me in extremely trying circumstances—in Air Force tents, rented apartments in Delhi, and Simla boarding-houses, until he died of cerebral malaria in 1944. Then with my mother and stepfather, life became even more chaotic, for they were perennially in debt, and had to shift (or be shifted) from house to house, so that the only fixed point for me was the large library, at Bishop Cotton School, Simla, where I lived for nine months in the year.

Now, when I see married people quarrel, I am full of fear and trepidation, for them and for their children. An unsettled childhood can give you a terrible sense of insecurity. Perhaps it's the real reason I never married. (Or fell into debt.)

I owe a lot to that school library, and to whoever left me in complete charge of it, for I had the keys and could go there at odd hours, ostensibly to catalogue the books but in reality to pore through them and become familiar with both the illustrious and the unfamiliar. In stolen moments over a period of three years, I read all the novels of Dickens, Stevenson, Jack London,

Hugh Walpole, J.B. Priestley, the Brontës (in no particular order), the complete plays of J. M. Barrie, Bernard Shaw, A.A. Milne, Somerset Maugham and Ben Travers, and the essays—and it was a great time for essayists—of A. G. Gardiner (*Alpha of the Plough*), Robert Lynd, Priestley again, Belloc, Chesterton and many others. And then, of course, there were the humorous writers—Mark Twain, Thurber, Wodehouse, Stephen Leacock, Jerome K. Jerome, W. W. Jacobs, Barry Pain, H. G. Wells (in his shorter works), Damon Runyon—I lapped them all up. My favourite humorous book, then and now, is *The Diary of a Nobody* by George and William Grossmith; it never fails to make me laugh, even though I must have read it over ten times. Five years ago, it cured me of a peptic ulcer.

As you can see, most of my reading was very English (even in content); but I did not come to an appreciation of Kipling until I was in my twenties, at which time I also made forays into the worlds of R. K. Narayan, Mulk Raj Anand, Rabindranath Tagore (in rather treacly translation) and a neglected autobiographical writer, Sudhin Ghose, whose books *And Gazelles Leaping* and *Cradle of the Clouds*, gave me great pleasure. The American short story writer, William Saroyan (*My Name Is Aaram* and many others), also strongly influenced me when I was starting out as a writer. So did André Gide. And so did the poetry of Walter de la Mare. My tastes may be old-fashioned but they are never out-of-date.

But those were writers. What of the people in my life? As a young man, I never had celebrities writing Forewords or Introductions to my books; I was really too proud to ask for them. Nor was I to experience a book being 'released' at a cocktail party until I had been writing for thirty-five years; writing was a lonely personal art and not an exercise in public relations.

But of course there were influences, and childhood influences are strongest.

My father's death when he was forty-six (and I was just ten), was a cruel blow of fate. It was a traumatic experience for me because I had been closest to him—practically his only companion during the last two or three years of his life—and

243

his death sent me even deeper into my cocoon of loneliness.

I had always been a shy boy, slow to make friends of my own age, and I was to remain a loner for the first thirty years of my life. Even after forty, when I became a provider for a family, I was given to solitary walks and periods of spiritual withdrawal. Which is the greater truth—that no man is an island, or that every man is an island? When I look at some of those large urban working-class families proliferating on the outskirts of Delhi or any large town, everyone eating and sleeping and screaming in one tiny flat, it is difficult to believe in 'islands' of individuality. But they are often kept together by force of circumstance. Remove one of those family members from his familiar habitat and leave him with the unfamiliar, and he will perhaps discover his identity and individuality. Most humans, gregarious by nature, are, by constant co-mingling with their fellows, able to shut out all thought of their 'island' identities; these are the ones who find it difficult to live with themselves, who hate being alone. Most of us are extroverts except on our death-beds!

And yet, it is equally true to say that no man is an island. Would I be half the writer I am today if I had not learnt to live with, and for, others?

'Why do you make yourself *suffer* so?' asked a wealthy Delhi socialite of me, not so long ago. 'You have taken on all these people, and now you are tied down—you are afraid to make a move because one is sick or another is unhappy. Why don't you learn to be *selfish*—like me?'

'That's just it,' I said. 'I *am* selfish—far more than you can ever be! I'm selfish because I want to be with those I love—all the time. I don't want to be away from them even for a day!' I was referring to Prem and his family—especially the children. And I remembered my father and how anxious he was to be with me all the time—from the moment he returned from work to the moment he set off again the next day. He was a sick man then, without any moral support, for he and my mother had separated two or three years previously. He was afraid that I might be taken from him too. He had no intention of giving me up. It was selfishness of the highest order.

My socialite friend has a son who is an alcoholic and a daughter who is a drug-addict. She has little or no time for them. They are worthless, according to her. She is probably right. So she refuses to suffer because of them! Or so she declares. It must take a strong will to harden one's heart against one's own flesh and blood. Is it only in TV serials or Bombay movies that mothers are spotless, sacrificing their all?

If I did not, as a child, receive the same love from my mother as I did from my father, it was not entirely her fault. As she had married again and was engaged in bringing up my stepbrothers, a clash of interests was only to be expected. A note of resentment creeps in here. I did resent stepfather, stepbrothers and the whole unwanted step-scene that I had to live with after my father's death. Writing was one way of getting away from it all! Looking back, I expect they did their best for me. My stepfather was a man without any imagination, and it just did not occur to him that a child might need more than food and clothing. My mother's sensuality was, I think, stronger than her intelligence. In me, sensuality and intelligence have been at war with each other almost all my life, and are even now at war.

*

As a youth, loneliness always went hand in hand with a powerful pull or attraction towards another person, be it boy or girl—and very often without that individual being aware of it. I think I expressed this feeling in a short poem, 'Passing By', which I wrote many years ago:

Enough for me that you are beautiful:
Beauty possessed diminishes.
Better a dream of love
Than love's dream broken;
Better a look exchanged
Than love's word spoken.
Enough for me that you walk past,
A firefly flashing in the dark.

245

It was probably written as a result of unrequited love. For, whenever I pursued a loved one, that person proved elusive. On the other hand, the most lasting relationships have been those that have grown slowly, without fret or frenzy. Declarations of passionate love or undying friendship are fine in their own way; but the important thing is to feel *comfortable* with someone, and not have to keep proving yourself in one way or another.

I was a good soccer goalkeeper—one of the few accomplishments that I forget to be modest about! And although my football-playing days ended when I left school, I have been a goalkeeper all my life—providing, protecting, defending home territory, rather than being an aggressive goal-scorer or go-getter; in other words, a stout defender rather than a dashing, flashy centre-forward. No, I never have been a dasher, and will never be one. It's been 'Tramp, tramp, tramp along the highway', in the words of an old Nelson Eddy favourite. An occasional high kick to feed the forwards can always be expected; the rest of the time I'm happy to use my good reflexes in protecting my citadel (crumbling though the walls of Ivy Cottage maybe), my loved ones, my way of life, and my privacy. And when I take to the open road, it's almost always on foot, seldom in a limousine.

If I write my autobiography it will, I think, be called *Writing For My Life*. Ever since I started freelancing, on my return from England in 1955, I have been writing in order to sustain the sort of life I like to lead—unhurried, evenpaced, sensual, in step with the natural world, most at home with humble people . . . . . I have never aspired to cars, houses, or even furniture. Property is for the superstitious. I have no assets except the books I have written and the few that may still be lurking in the innermost recesses of my mind. 'I give to the world that which is in my heart,' wrote the composer Franz Schubert, and I have tried to do the same. It should outlast the furniture.

My response to nature has been instinctive, but my attitudes have also been influenced by Thoreau's *Walden* and Richard Jefferies' *The Story of My Heart*. Jefferies' book is not simply a description of nature lore, it is a work of poetic and mystic vision. He was consumptive and he wrote in great poverty, but he wrote in the heightened consciousness that often came to those who suffered from tuberculosis.

There were many great writers who were consumptive: Sterne, Keats, the Brontës (Emily, Charlotte, Ann and Branwell), Thoreau, Stevenson, Poe, D.H. Lawrence, Katherine Mansfield, numerous others. Are there certain morbid conditions, tuberculosis being one, that intensify and accelerate the growth of a creative gift? The tendency to snatch at life, to sweep together greedily, all the sensations and impressions life offers, must have been characteristic of the consumptive temperament.

Jefferies was a solitary man, a quietist, an atheist, who did not move in literary circles. 'To reflect that another human being,' he wrote,

> if at a distance of ten thousand years from the year 1883, would enjoy one hour's more life, in the sense of fullness of life, in the consequence of anything I had done in my little span, would be to me a peace of soul.

I do not know about ten thousand years, but I can certainly say that one hundred years after Jefferies wrote those words, there was at least one reader, myself, who enjoyed many hours of delight in 'physical emotion' as a result of reading the work of one who was more a pagan than a gentle naturalist.

As the reader will by now have realized, books have been a passion with me all my life, quite literally taking the place of furniture, as they lie stacked up in places where most people keep their ornamental bric-a-brac. Forty years of reading and writing have made my eyesight very weak, and now I get headaches if I read or write for too long. But I am glad I was able to get through thousands of books before this happened. At a rough calculation, I must have read over 15,000 books in my lifetime. And now, when I do read, I like to go back to old favourites, just as we like to be among old friends as we get older and the going gets tough.

In a notebook kept in the 1950s, I had transcribed these words of Virginia Woolf, written in 1932:

> I have sometimes dreamt that when the Day of Judgement dawns and the great conquerors and lawyers and statesmen come to receive their rewards—their crowns, their laurels, their names carved indelibly upon imperishable marble—the Almighty will turn to Peter and will say, not without a certain envy when He sees us coming with our books under our arms, 'Look, these need no reward. We have nothing to give them here. They have loved reading.'

*

My first attempt at a novel or memoir was at school in Simla, when I was thirteen. It was called *Nine Months*, but had nothing to do with a pregnancy; it referred merely to the length of the school term, the beginning of March to the end of November, and it detailed my friendships, escapades, ambitions, and views on life in general, as well as describing the foibles of some of our masters. It filled two exercise books and lay in my desk for a couple of months, before it disappeared—pinched, no doubt, by an early collector of original manuscripts.

It was a sentimental account of school life, an extension of the diaries I had learnt to keep as a child. It had been my father, much earlier, who had encouraged me to keep a diary of sorts—and this I did in a desultory fashion during those long hot summer days in Delhi, while he was away at Air Headquarters and I lay on a cot beneath a ceiling-fan, waiting for the cool of the evening to bring him home. Then, when life became tolerable outside, he would take me to Connaught Place (quite new and glistening in 1943) to see a film or eat ice-cream at Wenger's or down milk-shakes at the Milk Bar. Those early diary entries were often just lists of books I had read or records I had bought or films I had seen (casts included), but they served to give me a good memory for detail and even today I can rattle off the cast of any film made in the 1940s, and not just the authors, but also the publishers of books brought out in the first half of this century. Yes, I read all the Hugh Lofting books, but I can also tell you that they were published by Jonathan Cape, and that William Saroyan's publishers were Faber and Faber, and that if anyone wrote a book about cats he'd find a sympathetic publisher in Michael Joseph!

This habit of keeping a diary did get me into trouble later on— not at school, but in my aunt's house in Jersey (in the Channel Islands) where I went to stay when, at the age of seventeen, I went to the UK. Some critical remarks about my relatives' diehard colonial attitudes were read by my uncle—who, unable to contain his curiosity, had dipped into my diary—and there was an awful row. I packed my suitcase and took the boat to Southampton, from where I journeyed up to London. That was when I wrote my first novel, *The Room on the Roof*.

I think I have always been pretty much in charge of my own life (made easier by the fact of not having any expectations from family of relatives)—leaving home to go to England, leaving Jersey to go to London, leaving London after three years and returning to India to freelance from Dehra and New Delhi; taking jobs when I had to, but always returning to my first love, which was full-time writing; leaving Delhi to live in the hills; and now, who knows, maybe it's time to move on again.

But all those early moves and decisions were taken when I was alone and unencumbered: living in that small attic room in north-west London and scribbling away at night, determined to get published; walking the streets of that great city until I discovered where almost every writer of note had lived, from Samuel Johnson to Hugh Walpole! And yet, I did not meet any living authors. Over the years, I have met very few writers. I seem to have been sustained by the ghosts of yesterday's greats.

And I needed that sustenance, for in a place like Dehra in the mid-Fifties, there were few if any literary influences and certainly no literary atmosphere. By day, I lived for my friendships and affairs; by night, I lived for my books and writing. It is difficult to write on a hot and humid afternoon;

better to use that time for sleeping or making love, and keep the nights free for literature!

But I must not forget my friend, William Matheson, a Swiss journalist, who lived in Dehra for a time. He would dissect and tear my stories to bits, and this had a salutary effect on my over-writing. His praise was so sparing, so rare, that when he did say something was good, I *knew* it was good.

It has not been very different these many years in the hill-station. The mountains are magic; but, let's face it, hill-stations are by now tawdry, tatty places, and Mussoorie is no exception. Tourism and private schools are its *raison d'être*. The odd writer has come this way but has usually hurried on elsewhere. I stayed on because of my personal relationships. It had nothing to do with my writing. Although I love to sit in the shade of a friendly chestnut tree, notebook on my knee, I can write just as well in a crowded railway compartment or seedy hotel veranda—and have frequently done so.

I live in simple, even austere conditions. Prem and the family have two small rooms, I have two small rooms. One of these is taken up by books and a few chairs for the occasional visitor. The other, smaller, is my bedroom-cum-study. It is bright and sunny, and the windows open out on the mountains and valley. There is a road below where people and vehicles pass by.

Most of the essays written since 1980 and included in this book, were written in this room. So were a number of my children's books. (The majority of my short stories belong to an earlier period.) Here I have written the odd poem, and here I listen to music, and here I talk to the children, and here I grow ivy on my walls. It is a good room for indoor plants, and I get on well with plants, particularly climbers.

There is an old and faded rug on the floor. My wooden bed has done service for twenty years. My typewriter has done service for forty years; it is used to my touch; it has acquired a soul and I wouldn't exchange it for a word-processor.

My books are old, my pictures are old, my shoes are old, my only suit is *very* old.

Only I am young.

Growing up was always a difficult process for me, and I gave up trying many years ago. I decided that there was little point in becoming an adult, if I could remain a child and still make a living.

I have the temper of a child, and a tendency to be mischievous. And I still retain a childlike trust in grown-ups, which sometimes works to my detriment. But it doesn't matter. In the long run, the exploiters and manipulators meet with their come-uppances; they are their own worst enemies.

I think I have remained young because I have always had children around me. Not just the children in my own family, but other children too. I love to watch them grow. Adolescence is a fascinating period and I keep going back to it in my fiction.

Raki, Muki, Dolly . . . . They have grown up under my roof, they are with me now, and God willing, they and their children will be with me when I die. If I finally close this window and leave this town for another place, they will go with me. If they grow up and go away, I will stay near them. That's what love is all about. Staying there, prepared to render service.

Most of my life I have given of myself, and in return I have received love in abundance. Life hasn't been a bed of roses. And yet, quite often, I've had roses out of season.

4 May 1993   *Ruskin Bond*
Mussoorie